As one of ... hed
... nds,
... vel.

... n of
... ssion for travel.

**Rely on Thomas Cook as your
travelling companion on your next trip
and benefit from our unique heritage.**

Thomas Cook **pocket** guides

SWANSEA

Written by Victoria Trott

Published by Thomas Cook Publishing
A division of Thomas Cook Tour Operations Limited
Company registration no. 3772199 England
The Thomas Cook Business Park, Unit 9, Coningsby Road,
Peterborough PE3 8SB, United Kingdom
Email: books@thomascook.com, Tel: +44 (0) 1733 416477
www.thomascookpublishing.com

Produced by Cambridge Publishing Management Limited
Burr Elm Court, Main Street, Caldecote CB23 7NU
www.cambridgepm.co.uk

ISBN: 978-1-84848-490-0

First edition © 2011 Thomas Cook Publishing
Text © Thomas Cook Publishing
Cartography supplied by Redmoor Design, Tavistock, Devon
Map data © OpenStreetMap contributors CC-BY-SA, www.openstreetmap.org,
www.creativecommons.org

Series Editor: Karen Beaulah
Production/DTP: Steven Collins

Printed and bound in Spain by GraphyCems

Cover photography © graham bell/Alamy

CONTENTS

INTRODUCING SWANSEA
Introduction 6
When to go 8
History 10
Culture 12

MAKING THE MOST OF SWANSEA
Shopping 14
Eating & drinking 16
Entertainment 18
Sport & relaxation 20
Accommodation 22
The best of Swansea 26
Suggested itineraries 28
Something for nothing 30
When it rains 31
On arrival 32

THE CITY OF SWANSEA
Introduction to city areas 40
The city centre 42
The waterfront 54
Swansea West 64

OUT OF TOWN TRIPS
Mumbles 74
The Gower Peninsula 80

PRACTICAL INFORMATION
Directory 90

INDEX 94

MAPS
Swansea 34
Swansea centre 41
Swansea region 81

SYMBOLS KEY
The following symbols are used throughout this book:

ⓐ address ☎ telephone ⓦ website address ⓔ email
🕐 opening times 🚊 public transport connections ❶ important

The following symbols are used on the maps:

🄸 information office		▮ point of interest	
✈ airport		O city	
✚ hospital		O large town	
🛡 police station		○ small town	
🚌 bus station		═ motorway	
🚉 railway station		— main road	
✉ post office		— minor road	
✝ church		— railway	
❶ numbers denote featured cafés, restaurants & venues			

PRICE CATEGORIES
The ratings below indicate average price rates for a double
room per night, including breakfast:
£ under £50 ££ £50–100 £££ over £100
The typical cost for a three-course meal without drinks,
is as follows:
£ under £20 ££ £20–30 £££ over £30

▶ *The spectacular Sail Bridge in the Maritime Quarter*

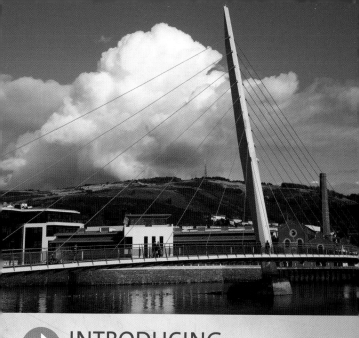

INTRODUCING
Swansea

Introduction

Its bay has been likened to that of Naples and its seven hills to those of Rome. For writer Dylan Thomas, the city's most famous son, it was 'an ugly, lovely town' and to Hollywood actress Catherine Zeta-Jones it's simply 'home'. Welcome to Swansea.

The city by the sea has come a long way since Sweyn the Viking supposedly settled on his ey (island). First along were the Normans, who recognised a good strategic location when they saw one, and left their mark with a castle and the origins of the city centre we know today. However, it was in the 19th century that Swansea really came into its own as the world centre for copper smelting and one of Britain's busiest ports.

Life moved on: industry declined, the docks – unable to receive larger ships – lay empty, and the city saw its darkest hour when it was flattened by bombing raids during World War II. Nonetheless, following the example of their Viking and Norman ancestors, the people of Swansea battled on.

Now, Wales's second city is a friendly, multicultural place with two wonderfully located universities and an ever-developing waterfront, which is home to a boating marina, the **National Waterfront Museum** and Wales's tallest building. A £4 million project aims to turn the waterfront into a world-class venue for sailing events. The grey and functional post-war city centre is now undergoing a £1 billion regeneration programme to attract major high-street brands, hotel chains and house builders.

To find the city's soul, wander around the stalls in Wales's largest indoor market, have a drink down **Wind Street** on a

Saturday night or head to the **Liberty Stadium** – home of Ospreys Rugby and Swansea City Football Club – on match day.

But Swansea isn't just a city; it's a bay and the gateway to the **Gower Peninsula** – Britain's first designated Area of Outstanding Natural Beauty. Three miles from the city centre is the lovely former fishing village of **Mumbles**, now one of the most desirable coastal residential locations in the country.

So perhaps that's why Dylan Thomas called Swansea the 'graveyard of ambition' – come here and you will never want to leave!

◆ *The National Waterfront Museum opened in 2005*

When to go

SEASONS & CLIMATE

Swansea is a year-round destination, with attractions to interest all members of the family, but if you come in spring and summer, when the temperature averages 20°C (64°F), it will be the best time to make the most of the area's wonderful beaches, coastal walks and outdoor events. The wettest months are generally October to January; however, be prepared for rain at any time – Swansea is officially Britain's wettest city.

ANNUAL EVENTS

From dance music to literature and from beer to gardens: whatever floats your boat, you're sure to find something to suit in Swansea's varied events calendar.

The year really gets going at the end of February with **Saint David's Week** (ⓦ www.saintdavidsday.com), which celebrates Wales's patron saint with a food and drink festival, music concerts by Welsh artists and free Welsh classes for beginners.

The events that take place from May to September collectively make up **Swansea Bay Summer Festival** (ⓦ www. swanseabay festival.com). Clyne Gardens shows off its azaleas and rhododendrons during **Clyne in Bloom** (ⓦ www. breatheswansea. com). Also in May, **Swansea Bay Film Festival** (ⓦ www.swansea filmfestival.com) showcases the work of experimental and independent film-makers from around the world.

June sees two events in Singleton Park for the city's more flamboyant inhabitants. **Escape into the Park** (ⓦ www.escapefestival.com) is Wales's biggest annual dance event, where top international DJs attract revellers from far and wide, while drag queens and pop poppets entertain gay revellers at **Swansea Pride** (Ⓦ www.swanseapride.com).

In August, communities from all around the world celebrate their music, dance and food in Museum Park during **World Party Weekend** and real ale lovers flock to the Brangwyn Hall for **Swansea Bay Beer Festival** (Ⓦ www.swanseacamra.org.uk). Singleton Botanical Gardens also has its **Botanics in Bloom** festival in August. Athletic sorts descend upon the city in September to run along the seafront in the **Admiral Swansea Bay 10K** (Ⓦ www.swanseabay10k.com).

The Dylan Thomas Festival (Ⓦ www.dylanthomas.com) celebrates the life and work of Swansea's legendary scribe at the end of October and in the same month **Swansea Festival of Music and the Arts** (Ⓦ www.swanseafestival.org) is a must for fans of opera, classical music and dance. The year ends with ice-skating and festive fun at **Waterfront Winterland** (Ⓦ www.waterfrontwinterland.com) from mid-November.

⬣ Swansea's wide expanse of beach

History

It's a surprise to learn that Swansea only became a city in 1969, particularly when you consider how it led both Wales and the world in several ways in the 19th century: it was the location of Wales's first purpose-built cinema, first museum and first national daily newspaper; it gave the world its first railway passenger service, later known as the Mumbles Train; and two of the city's inhabitants, John Dillwyn Llewelyn and the Reverend Calvert Richard Jones, were early pioneers of photography.

It was due to Swansea's coastal location and natural assets that it created all this innovation and attracted investment. Thanks to the River Tawe and an abundance of coal, the Lower Swansea Valley became the world centre for copper production in the 19th century. Copper ore was brought from as far as Chile

⬣ *Pleasure boats dock at Swansea nowadays*

and Cuba direct to the works on the banks of the Tawe, where local coal was used to fire the furnaces to smelt the ore into copper. The final product was then exported. In the 1860s, Carl Wilhelm Siemens developed the open-hearth furnace here to produce steel; his company became the world's fourth largest steel producer.

Swansea's most difficult period came during World War II. The city suffered heavy bombing on a number of occasions, most notably during the 'Three Night Blitz' of 19–21 February 1941, when most of the city centre was flattened; the area was a prized target due to its port and nearby oil refinery.

The city was rebuilt in the 1950s and continues to move onwards and upwards. Where there was heavy industry, there are now enterprise parks; the docks house pleasure boats instead of copper barques and the few remaining warehouses accommodate restaurants and galleries. Swansea continues to make its contribution to the world via research and development in the fields of medicine, science and technology.

THE CAPE HORNERS

The 'Cape Horners' were sailors who went to Chile to fetch copper ore, a dangerous journey – which involved rounding the infamous headland – from which many never returned. Swansea's sailors were the most successful 'Cape Horners' and were highly regarded. The most famous copper barque was *Zeta*, from which Catherine Jones got her exotic middle name.

Culture

Swansea has four museums where visitors can discover the essence of the city: **Swansea Museum**, for local archaeology; the **Glynn Vivian Art Gallery**, for Swansea pottery; the **Dylan Thomas Centre**, for the man and his work; and the **National Waterfront Museum**, for the city's industrial heritage.

There are three theatres: the 19th-century **Grand Theatre**, which mainly stages national touring productions and comedy but also has art exhibitions in its Arts Wing; the **Dylan Thomas Theatre**, home to Swansea Little Theatre; and the **Taliesin Arts Centre**, whose focus is dance, plays and arthouse films. The multi-screen Odeon and Vue cinemas show the latest blockbusters.

A year-round events calendar ensures that there's something to suit everyone, especially music lovers, with everything from opera to jazz and from folk to dance; Monkey, The Chattery and Milkwoodjam are popular independent live music venues.

The work of Dylan Thomas is celebrated each year with a festival at the end of October, and the city hosts the world's biggest literary prize for young writers, The Dylan Thomas Prize, every year in December.

▶ *The bar of Swansea's famed Morgans Hotel*

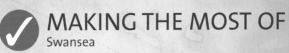

MAKING THE MOST OF
Swansea

Shopping

Although Swansea is the main shopping centre for those living in southwest Wales, it has always been in the shadow of Cardiff, its easterly neighbour. But that is starting to change. The city centre, virtually unaltered since its post-war rebuild in the 1950s, is now undergoing a £1 billion regeneration programme, which is adding new retail units as well as accommodation, hotels, offices and leisure facilities.

Gone is the much-loved David Evans House of Fraser store, and in its place is a shiny new glass-fronted outlet whose current occupants include Zara and Slaters Menswear. The city's main shopping area is on and around **Oxford Street**, where H&M and Top Shop eye Marks & Spencer and Next. The **Quadrant Shopping Centre** has all your shopping needs under one roof, as it is here you'll find Debenhams, Boots and WH Smith.

The jewel in the crown is **Swansea Indoor Market** (Ⓦ www.swanseaindoormarket.co.uk), which is Wales's largest indoor market. Famed for its Welsh cakes, fish, and cockle and laverbread stalls, it's also a good place to look for jewellery, postcards and Welsh-themed gifts.

Up on **The Kingsway**, best known for its nightclubs, is Swansea's designer mecca, Moda. Here you'll find the likes of Emporio Armani, Hugo Boss and D&G; they've got a nice café-bar too. A bit further west is **St Helen's Road**, which is lined with ethnic food shops and restaurants. Students living in Uplands and Brynmill won't starve, as the main drag, **Uplands Crescent**, is dotted with cafés and takeaways as well as a supermarket.

The eastern side of town is home to **Parc Tawe Retail Park**, built on the site of the old North Dock. Staples, Homebase and clothing retailers are based here, while Sainsbury's sits nearby in the shadow of the Sail Bridge. **The waterfront** has some nice art galleries and jewellery designers.

The popular Quadrant Shopping Centre

Eating & drinking

To find out what Swansea eats, head to the Indoor Market, where you'll discover the best local produce under one roof. The sweet smell of Welsh cakes sizzling on the griddle is sure to get the taste buds tingling, as is the sight of legs of saltmarsh lamb, direct from the Burry Estuary. The mounds of Gower-grown potatoes, cauliflower and swede are a feast for the eyes, while sea bass is one of the treasures found in the area's waters. Look out for mackerel, too, in August.

Fresh Gower Cockles

⬣ Cockles and laverbread are a local speciality

The sweet of tooth have two treats in store: Kate Jones's award-winning chocolate brownies (ⓦ www.gowercottage brownies.com) are sold in cafés in Swansea and Gower, while Joe's ice cream (ⓦ www.joes-icecream.com) is a local institution and has been made in the city since 1922; the creamy vanilla is the most popular, but Welsh-cake flavour is also worth a lick.

Gourmet or takeaway, you'll find it in Swansea. There are restaurants of all kinds – French, Thai, Chinese, Italian, vegetarian – but Wind Street is a good place to head if you're short on time as it's here you'll find the big-name chains; the best Indian restaurants are found on St Helen's Road. On sunny days, take a picnic to one of the city's parks – watch out for the squirrels in Singleton! – or relax on a beachfront bench. Better still, take the bus out to Rhossili: in 2010 the Downs were voted Britain's best picnic spot by the British Guild of Travel Writers.

A TASTE OF THE SEA

In the centre of the Indoor Market, you won't be able to miss the piles of plump yellow shellfish and the cellophane-wrapped black goo on display, otherwise known as cockles and laverbread. Cockles have been farmed in the Burry Estuary off North Gower for generations and are traditionally eaten with fried bacon and laverbread, a kind of seaweed purée that is often sprinkled with oatmeal.

Entertainment

As a port, Swansea has had plenty of visitors over the centuries and provides lots of entertainment for them, from pubs to music halls. One remnant from the past is the flatiron-shaped Palace Theatre near the train station, which is one of only two purpose-built 19th-century music halls left in the UK. Now disused, its future is uncertain as it is currently up for sale.

These days, people from far and wide fill the bars and clubs of Wind Street most weeknights; it is pedestrianised at the weekend. The Kingsway has Wales's largest nightclub, **Oceana**, which hosts major dance music events. There's a thriving live music scene, whether you're into jazz, blues, indie or rock, and as well as venues in the centre of town, there's also a cluster in Uplands. The Liberty Stadium occasionally stages concerts by big-name artists. Add to these three theatres, two multi-screen cinemas and a ten-pin bowling alley, not forgetting the wide variety of restaurants, and there's no need to find yourself at a loose end on any night of the week. A stroll around the marina or along the prom on a warm summer's evening will prove that the best things in life are undoubtedly free.

Tickets for the cinema, theatre or musical performances are available directly from the venue box offices. **Derrick's Music** (ⓐ 221 Oxford Street ⓣ 01792 654226 ⓦ www.derricksmusic-shop.co.uk) sells tickets for gigs in Swansea, Cardiff and Bristol.

To find out what's on, pick up a copy of the free monthly *What's On* magazine from the tourist office (ⓐ Plymouth Street ⓣ 01792 468321 ⓦ www.visitswanseabay.com/events). *Buzz* (ⓦ www.buzzmag.co.uk), another free monthly mag, lists arts and music events across South Wales and can also be found at the tourist office. Also check out the website of the local newspaper, *South Wales Evening Post* (ⓦ www.thisissouthwales. co.uk/entertainment).

🔺 *The Grand Theatre has been entertaining people since 1897*

Sport & relaxation

Swansea is passionate about both rugby union and football. In 2005, the Ospreys and Swans moved from their respective homes at St Helen's and the Vetch Field to the new Liberty Stadium – Wales's third largest stadium – in Landore. Glamorgan Cricket Club, whose headquarters are in Cardiff, also often play cricket at the St Helen's ground near the university, and it was at this ground that Sir Garfield Sobers hit the first-ever 6 sixes in one over (six balls) in 1968. Whether you want to sit back and watch or actively take part, you'll find something to suit in Swansea.

SPECTATOR SPORTS

Both the **Ospreys** (ⓦ www.ospreysrugby.com) and **Swansea City Football Club** (ⓦ www.swanseacity.net) play at the **Liberty Stadium**. ⓐ The Liberty Stadium, Landore ⓣ 08700 400004 ⓦ www.liberty-stadium.com ⓝ Bus: X20, 120, 125

Both **Glamorgan Cricket Club** (ⓣ 029 2041 9311 ⓦ www. glamorgancricket.com) and **Swansea RFC** (ⓣ 01792 424242 ⓦ www.swansearfc.co.uk) play at St Helen's. ⓐ St Helen's, Bryn Road ⓝ Bus: 2, 2A, 2B, 2C, 3, 3A

PARTICIPATION SPORTS
Golf
Ashleigh Road Pitch & Putt is a ten-hole golf course where you don't need a handicap and can hire equipment on site. ⓐ Blackpill, Oystermouth Road ⓣ 01792 207544 ⓝ Bus: 2, 2A, 2B, 2C, 3, 3A

Swimming, watersports and fitness

The **Wales National Pool** is an Olympic-size swimming pool that is open to the public for lengths, aqua fitness, or splash and play sessions for kids. ⓐ Sketty Lane ⓣ 01792 513513 ⓦ www.walesnationalpoolswansea.co.uk ⓝ Bus: 2, 2A, 2B, 2C, 3, 3A

The LC is the new name of the revamped leisure centre, offering pools and slides, a surf machine, exercise classes, a sports hall, a climbing wall, a spa and a children's play area. ⓐ Oystermouth Road ⓣ 01792 466500 ⓦ www.thelcswansea. com ⓛ Term: 16.00–21.00 Mon–Fri, 09.00–20.00 Sat & Sun (see website for full listings)

Swansea Watersports offers sailing, kayaking, power-boating, windsurfing and jet-skiing for beginners and experts. ⓣ 07989 839878 ⓦ www.swanseawatersports.com

Tennis

Victoria Park has four outdoor municipal courts by Swansea Bay. ⓐ Guildhall Road ⓣ 01792 635411 ⓝ Bus: 2, 2A, 2B, 2C, 3, 3A

🔺 *The pool at the LC*

Accommodation

Whatever kind of accommodation you're looking for, you're sure to find it in Swansea. The city centre and eastern approach road have their fair share of chain hotels: Ibis (ⓐ Fabian Way ❶ 01792 638800 ⓦ www.ibishotel.com), Marriott (ⓐ Maritime Quarter ❶ 01792 642020 ⓦ www.marriott.co.uk), Premier Inn (ⓐ Salubrious Place ❶ 0871 527 9060 ⓦ www.premierinn.com), Travelodge (ⓐ Princess Way ❶ 0871 984 6326 ⓦ www.travelodge.co.uk) and Village (ⓐ Fabian Way ❶ 0844 847 2970 ⓦ www.village-hotels.co.uk). However, it's worth checking a price comparison website such as ⓦ www.travelsupermarket.com before booking direct.

Uplands is where you'll find most of the city's B&B accommodation – Oystermouth Road is the place to look for budget options. Many of the city's new apartments, especially in the Maritime Quarter, provide attractive self-catering options.

The only hostel in the area is a YHA one out on Gower, but the university offers both B&B and self-catering from July to September (❶ 01792 295665 ⓦ www.swansea.ac.uk/conferences). The Tourist Information Centre (see page 93) has a bed-booking service if you arrive in town with nowhere to stay.

A few miles out of town, Mumbles and the Gower Peninsula have everything from luxury hotels and stylish restaurants-with-rooms to basic campsites and B&Bs in scenic locations.

HOTELS
Windsor Lodge ££ At this comfortable, cosy hotel in a Georgian building near Swansea Metropolitan University, the welcoming

lounge has a contemporary yet homely feel and the bedrooms a shabby-chic air. Smoked kippers feature on the breakfast menu. ⓐ Mount Pleasant ⓣ 01792 648996 ⓦ www.windsor-lodge.co.uk

The Dragon ££–£££ Slap bang in the city centre, this 1960s high-rise hotel has undergone a £3.7 million facelift in recent years and now offers 106 bright, contemporary rooms, a health and fitness suite with a pool and spa and an award-winning restaurant. ⓐ The Kingsway ⓣ 01792 657100 ⓦ www.dragon-hotel.co.uk

The Grand ££–£££ Opposite the train station, this renovated 1930s hotel is a good option for early starts or late arrivals. Rooms have contemporary décor in muted tones and the two penthouse suites boast rooftop hot tubs. ⓐ Ivey Place, High Street ⓣ 01792 645898 ⓦ www.thegrandhotelswansea.co.uk

Morgans ££–£££ Swansea's flagship hotel is in one of the city's most attractive buildings – the Grade II listed former Harbour Trust HQ. The luxurious and stylish rooms, named after the old copper barques (yes, there's a 'Zeta'), are popular with visiting celebrities who are reputed to enjoy a glass or two in the Champagne Bar. The hotel's nearby Georgian Townhouse offers a slightly more affordable night's stay. ⓐ Somerset Place ⓣ 01792 484848 ⓦ www.morganshotel.co.uk

The Towers ££–£££ Although situated 8 km (5 miles) outside Swansea, this modern hotel is very popular with visiting businesspeople and national and international rugby teams. Its 19th-century tower folly has been converted into three stunning suites and its spa and pool are arguably the finest in the area. ⓐ Jersey Marine ⓣ 01792 814155 ⓦ www.towershotel.co.uk ⓝ Bus: 156, 158

BED & BREAKFAST

The Beachcomber £–££ This cheap and cheerful guesthouse overlooks Swansea Bay. Rooms at the front can be noisy due to the proximity of the road. There are pancakes on the breakfast menu and even bacon sarnies. ⓐ 364 Oystermouth Road ⓣ 01792 651380 ⓦ www.beachcomberguesthouse.com ⓝ Bus: 2, 2A, 2B, 3, 3A, 3B

Leonardo's £–££ Another budget seafront option where light sleepers should opt for a room at the back. Foodies can try cockles and laverbread and vegetarians won't go hungry. There's free Wi-Fi too. ⓐ 380 Oystermouth Road ⓣ 01792 470163 ⓦ www.leonardosguesthouse.co.uk ⓝ Bus: 2, 2A, 2B, 3, 3A, 3B

The Alexander ££ A light and airy B&B, this is an ideal base for a weekend away. Some rooms overlook Swansea Bay and there's a games room where you can shoot some pool or throw some arrows. ⓐ 3 Sketty Road, Uplands ⓣ 01792 470045 ⓦ www.alexander-hotel.co.uk ⓝ Bus: 20, 20A, 21, 22, 37

The White House ££ This Victorian villa is instantly recognisable by the wonderful plants and flowers outside. Rooms are light and clean, dogs are welcome and the restaurant is renowned

for its use of local produce. ⓐ 4 Nyanza Terrace, Uplands
ⓣ 01792 473856 ⓦ www.thewhitehouse-hotel.com ⓝ Bus: 20,
20A, 21, 22, 37

The Mirador Town House ££–£££ The décor of the seven rooms
in this B&B are inspired by the four corners of the globe – The
French Connection has its own roof terrace and The Oriental
Pearl has its own lounge. Whichever you choose, there's free
Wi-Fi. ⓐ 14 Mirador Crescent, Uplands ⓣ 01792 466976
ⓦ www.themirador.co.uk ⓝ Bus: 20, 20A, 21, 22, 37

SELF-CATERING

Home from Home £–£££ From stylish apartments in the
Maritime Quarter to historic thatched cottages in the heart
of Gower, this lettings agency has the widest choice of self-
catering accommodation in the area. ⓐ 42 Queen's Road,
Mumbles ⓣ 01792 360624 ⓦ www.homefromhome.com

Dylan Thomas Birthplace ££ The house where Dylan Thomas
grew up and wrote most of his poetry has been restored
to its former glory, complete with 1914 décor, and offers
B&B and self-catering accomodation. ⓐ 5 Cwmdonkin Drive,
Uplands ⓣ 01792 405331 ⓦ www.5cwmdonkindrive.com
ⓝ Bus: 20, 20A, 21, 22, 37

A Space in the City ££–£££ Offers serviced accommodation in
some of Swansea's swankiest apartment blocks, including
Wales's highest building, for both business and leisure visitors.
ⓣ 0845 607050 ⓦ www.aspaceinthecity.co.uk

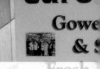

THE BEST OF SWANSEA

Swansea has something to offer visitors of all ages and interests, whatever time of year they decide to visit. Here are some of the places and experiences that should be at the top of everyone's list.

TOP 10 ATTRACTIONS

- **National Waterfront Museum** Learn all about Swansea and Wales's industrial and maritime past in this contemporary museum which opened in 2005 (see page 58).

- **Clyne Gardens** Admire the internationally renowned collection of rhododendrons and azaleas in one of the finest gardens in Wales (see page 64).

- **Dylan Thomas Centre** Learn about the life and work of Swansea's most famous son (see page 57).

- **Mumbles** Stroll around the charming former fishing village that Catherine Zeta-Jones calls 'home' (see page 74).

- **Rhossili** Marvel at the view of Worm's Head from the place that has been voted Britain's best beach and best picnic spot (see pages 82–3).

- **Joe's Ice Cream** Savour some of the best vanilla ice cream you'll find anywhere (see page 69).

- **Surfing** Ride the waves in Llangennith – Wales's answer to Malibu (see pages 82 and 86).

- **Swansea Indoor Market** Discover the area's best local produce in the largest indoor market in Wales (see pages 48–9).

- **The Promenade walk** Stroll or cycle the length – 8 km (5 miles) – of Swansea Bay from the Maritime Quarter to Mumbles (ⓦ www.swanseaprom.com) (see page 54).

- **Cockles and laverbread** Don't leave town without trying cockles accompanied by laverbread fried with salty bacon (see page 17).

⬇ *A seafood stall in the Indoor Market*

Suggested itineraries

HALF-DAY: SWANSEA IN A HURRY

Check out the castle ruins then turn right into Wind Street – one of the few areas of Swansea to escape destruction during World War II – and admire the Flemish-style architecture, before learning about Swansea's industrial heritage at the National Waterfront Museum. Stroll east through the marina and cross the Sail Bridge to the new SA1 development for lunch in one of the cafés or restaurants in the Grade-II-listed J-Shed and The Ice House.

1 DAY: TIME TO SEE A LITTLE MORE

Once you've spent the morning on the waterfront, take a bus to Singleton Park which, as well as offering plenty of green space, a boating lake and stunning views over the bay, has a renowned collection of rare and exotic tropical plants in its Botanical Gardens. Stroll back to the city centre along the Promenade, stopping en route for a delicious ice cream at Joe's (ⓐ 85 St Helen's Road). In the evening, enjoy a show at the Grand Theatre or take your pick from one of Swansea's wide variety of restaurants.

2–3 DAYS: SHORT CITY-BREAK

When you've spent a day exploring the city's delights, take the No 3 bus down to the former fishing village of Mumbles, sometime home of Hollywood actress Catherine Zeta-Jones. Browse the quirky boutiques and galleries on Newton Road, then head to PA's, which was recently voted Swansea's best restaurant, for lunch; later, take an exhilarating trip by speedboat around the coast or enjoy a gentle stroll through the Nature Reserve. On another day, buy supplies from Swansea Market and take the Gower Explorer bus out to Rhossili to savour a picnic in these beautiful surroundings. Energetic sorts will find plenty of activities on offer, from surfing to horse riding and from mountain boarding to bushcraft.

LONGER: ENJOYING SWANSEA TO THE FULL

The **National Botanic Garden of Wales** (ⓐ Llanarthne ⓣ 01558 668768 ⓦ www.gardenofwales.org.uk) is a 30-minute drive away and nearby **Afan Forest Park** (known locally as Afan Argoed) (ⓐ Port Talbot ⓣ 01639 850564 ⓦ www.afanforestpark. co.uk) is not only one of the world's best destinations for mountain biking but also a great place for walks.

🔺 *Autumn colours at Singleton Park Botanical Gardens*

Something for nothing

They say that the best things in life are free and that's certainly the case in Swansea. It doesn't cost a penny to stroll along the Promenade, relax on a sandy beach, admire the wonderful views from the top of Constitution Hill or explore one of the city's lovely gardens. All of Swansea's museums are free to the public, so there's no excuse to leave without learning all about the city's industrial heritage, sought-after pottery or the writer Dylan Thomas. Sir Frank Brangwyn's British Empire Panels, originally created for the House of Lords, are well worth a look in the Brangwyn Hall.

The city has a year-long events calendar and some of the festivities, such as World Party Weekend in August (see page 9). The Grand Theatre Arts Wing hosts free exhibitions by local artists. Free guides, including 'Walking and Cycling in Rural Swansea', are available from the Tourist Information Centre or from the tourist website (ⓦ www.visitswanseabay.com). Further afield, the nature reserves of Mumbles and Gower are all free of charge and the National Trust shop in Rhossili has details of walks on their property, which you can download from their website if you prefer (ⓦ www.nationaltrust.org.uk).

When it rains

John Wesley, founder of the Methodist movement, wrote during a visit to Swansea in August 1758, 'I scarce ever saw such rain in Europe as we had for a considerable part of this morning.' Well, things aren't always that bad, but the weather in Swansea certainly does have its moments, so thankfully there's plenty to do when the storm clouds have gathered. Much of the city's shopping area is under cover thanks to an indoor mall, two arcades and covered walkways. **The LC**, the city's revamped leisure centre (see page 21), has plenty to occupy all members of the family when you can't get to the beach, as does **Plantasia** (⊜ Parc Tawe ☎ 01792 474555 ⏱ 10.00–17.00 daily ⓘ Admission charge) with its tropical plants and exotic animals. Two multi-screen cinemas, **Odeon** and **Vue** (see page 53), show the latest films, while **Tenpin Bowling** (⊜ Parc Tawe ⓦ www.tenpin.co.uk) has 28 lanes and three American pool tables.

GOING UNDERGROUND

Deep in the Swansea Valley, the **National Showcaves Centre for Wales** was voted Britain's finest natural wonder in a Channel 5 competition. Dan-Yr-Ogof was the first cave discovered, but there are now two others – Bone Cave, where 42 human skeletons dating back to the Bronze Age have been found, and Cathedral Cave. ⊜ Abercrave ☎ 01639 730284 ⓦ www.showcaves.co.uk ⏱ 10.00–15.00 daily (Easter–Oct) 🚌 Bus: X63 ⓘ Admission charge

On arrival

ARRIVING

By air and/or rail

Unless you have a private jet (in which case you can land at the small airport on Gower), Swansea's nearest airport is Cardiff Airport (see page 90), which is 67 km (42 miles) away. It's mainly used by package tour companies and budget airlines, including bmibaby and Flybe, and primarily serves airports in the north of England, Ireland, Scotland and Europe. From the airport, you'll need to take a train (hourly) or bus (X91, every two hours) to Cardiff and change for a train (hourly) or bus (infrequent) to Swansea. Taxis stop outside the arrivals hall and can be booked in advance (❶ 01446 711747 ⓦ www.checkercars.com); a one-way trip to Swansea for up to four people costs around £70. All in all, if you're flying into Cardiff Airport, it's easiest to get a train or taxi or indeed hire a car – check out ⓦ www.travelsupermarket. com to compare prices.

The nearest international airport is Heathrow (❶ 0844 335 1801 ⓦ www.heathrowairport.com). Take the First Great Western train to London (see Directory) then hop on the Heathrow Express or Heathrow Connect, or get off at Reading for the RailAir Coach; you should book well in advance or travel off peak to get the cheapest tickets. There is a direct bus from Swansea to Heathrow with National Express (see Directory).

By car

By car, departing from the southeast, drive straight down the M4, and coming from the north down the M5, to Bristol, where you'll cross the Severn Bridge. The toll for the bridge is only payable in the westward direction (☏ 01454 633522 🌐 www.severnbridge.co.uk). Exit the M4 at Junction 42 on to Fabian Way for Swansea. There are three Park & Ride sites situated off main roads to the north (A4067), east (A483) and northwest (A483) of the city centre. There are 18 municipal car parks in the city centre, which are free on Sundays, plus multi-storeys at High Street, Rutland Street and Wellington Street. NCP (☏ 0845 050 7080 🌐 www.ncp.co.uk) has a car park at the train station and at Orchard Street, Salubrious Place and The Kingsway; parking is free for the first hour in Salubrious Place. The city is well signposted and you'll notice that signs are bilingual (English and Welsh).

◭ *A bilingual signpost at Swansea Marina*

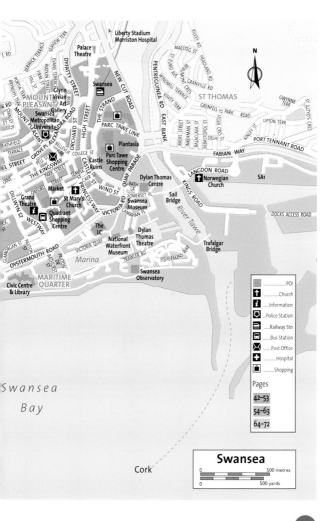

Liberty Stadium
Morriston Hospital

Palace Theatre

Swansea

Glynn
Vivian
Art
Gallery
Swansea
Metropolitan
University

ST THOMAS

Plantasia

Parc Tawe
Shopping
Centre
Castle
Ruins

Market

Grand
Theatre

St Mary's
Church

Quadrant
Shopping
Centre

The
LC

National
Waterfront
Museum

Civic Centre
& Library

MARITIME
QUARTER

Marina

Dylan Thomas
Centre

Swansea
Museum

Norwegian
Church

SA1

DOCKS ACCESS ROAD

Dylan
Thomas
Theatre

Sail
Bridge

Trafalgar
Bridge

Swansea
Observatory

River Tawe

Swansea
Bay

Cork

	POI
	Church
	Information
	Police Station
	Railway Stn
	Bus Station
	Post Office
	Hospital
	Shopping

Pages

42–53

54–63

64–72

Swansea

0   500 metres
0   500 yards

By coach

National Express links Swansea with other parts of the UK by coach and there's a new Greyhound bus service between Swansea and Cardiff (see Directory page 91).

By ferry

The Swansea–Cork ferry (see Directory page 91). There are four weekly overnight services in each direction in July and August and three weekly services during the rest of the year. Prices start at around £45 for a foot passenger and around £90 for a car and driver in July and August.

FINDING YOUR FEET

The city centre and waterfront are small enough to get around on foot; you might want to take a bus if you're going to SA1, Uplands or the university. The main approach to the city by bus and car is from the east along Fabian Way. The train station is at the top of High Street and a new bus station at the back of the Quadrant Shopping Centre opened in 2010. Like many cities, car crime is not unknown in Swansea so it's best to leave your vehicle in a secure car park and lock away valuables. Alcohol-related incidents can occur in the city's partying areas – Wind Street and The Kingsway – at the weekend. However, people in Swansea are generally well known for their friendliness.

ORIENTATION

Due to its small size, it would be difficult to get lost in Swansea; all you need to remember is that the hills are in the north, the waterfront is in the south, the university is west and the M4 is east. The city centre is surrounded by Oystermouth Road, Wind Street, The Kingsway (one way – west only) and West Way; this is where most of the traffic flows. The eastern end of Oxford Street is pedestrianised and the market is in the heart of the city. Uplands is a 20-minute walk from the city centre along Walter Road.

GETTING AROUND
By bus
The main ways to get around Swansea are on foot and by bus. A new bus station has just been built at the back of the Quadrant Shopping Centre and is now open. There are regular services to the university, Mumbles and Gower and tickets can be bought from the bus driver; it's a good idea to have coins available rather than notes. Traveline Cymru (ⓣ 0871 200 2233 ⓦ www.traveline-cymru.info) has information on all forms of public transport in Swansea and throughout the rest of Wales.

Taxis
Taxis can be found across the city (see page 91).

TOP BUS TRAVEL TIP
If you want to make more than one bus journey in a day, ask the bus driver for a 'FirstDay Swansea Bay' ticket, which gives unlimited travel around Swansea, Mumbles and Gower (valid on X18 service only for Gower).
See ⓦ www.firstcymru.co.uk for details.

● *One of Swansea's purple bendy buses*

By bike

Swansea offers many safe and wonderful opportunities for cycling, whether you want to breathe in the sea air along the Promenade, take the **Tawe Tour** alongside the river or head across country to Gower – there's even the **Gower Cycling Festival** in September. The tourist office publishes a leaflet, 'Walking and Cycling in Rural Swansea' – available from the Tourist Information Centre or on their website (see page 93). The City and County of Swansea (Ⓦ www.swansea.gov.uk/cycling) has a map of cycle parking sites, and cycling charity **Sustrans** (Ⓦ www.sustrans. org.uk) is also worth checking out.

Car hire

You don't really need a car to explore Swansea and Mumbles but one can be useful to get around the area. All the major car hire companies have offices here (see Directory page 92).

▶ *The elegant interior of the Glynn Vivian Art Gallery*

THE CITY OF
Swansea

Introduction to city areas

Bordered by hills in the north, the sea in the south and the university in the west, Swansea has been divided into three distinct areas for the purposes of this guidebook.

The **city centre**, compact and easily walkable, is where you'll find Swansea's main shopping area, including Wales's largest indoor market. Wind Street, one of the few parts of Swansea to escape bombing during World War II, is the place to go for bars and restaurants.

The second area covered is **the waterfront**. Here, once-busy docks have been transformed over the past 30 years into an attractive leisure and residential quarter. As well as swish apartments, this area is also where you'll find the boating marina and three of the city's museums.

Swansea West is where the university is located, overlooking the sea, about a mile and a half from the city centre. This is surrounded by Uplands and Brynmill, which are where most of Swansea's student population lives; this area is also the location of the city's lovely parks.

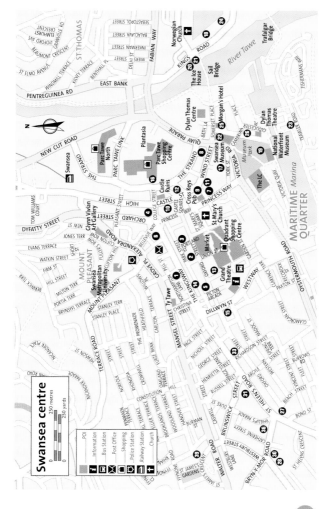

The city centre

Accessed from the east by car and from the north by train, Swansea's city centre caters for most needs. Shops are mainly of the high-street variety, while the Indoor Market showcases local produce. Night owls won't be disappointed – Swansea is well known for its after-dark offerings centred around Wind Street – and neither will foodies as the city has a wide variety of restaurants, some of which are national award winners. Culture vultures can take their pick from opera, ballet or plays at the 19th-century Grand Theatre and admire the fine collection of Cambrian Pottery at the Glynn Vivian Art Gallery.

SIGHTS & ATTRACTIONS

Castle ruins

There's been a castle atop the hill overlooking the mouth of the Tawe Estuary since the 11th century, when the Normans built a motte and bailey structure to protect the Marcher lords of Gower from attacks by the Welsh and English. The remains we see today, mainly a south-facing stone wall and tower, date from the 13th century. ❸ Opposite Castle Square

Castle Square

A circular, pedestrianised space with amphitheatre-style seating where a big screen occasionally shows sports and a stage is erected several times a year to host outdoor events. Look out for Amber Hiscott's sail-shaped glass leaf sculpture, inspired by one of Dylan Thomas's poems.

◆ Swansea Castle's remaining wall and tower

BIRTHPLACE OF A DANDY
Eighteenth-century dandy Beau Nash was born plain
Richard in a house next to the Cross Keys in 1674. The
'Master of Ceremonies' of Bath and, later, Tunbridge Wells,
Nash was responsible for turning both spa towns into the
most fashionable destinations of the day. The half-
timbered building that runs the length of Caer Street,
opposite Castle Square, is called Beau Nash House.

Cross Keys pub
Dating back to 1332, this is Swansea's oldest building after the
castle. It was originally built as a hospice but records show that
there has been an inn on the site since the 17th century.
🅐 12 St Mary Street ☎ 01792 630921 🆆 www.oxkeys.com
🕐 11.00–23.00 Mon–Sat, 12.00–22.30 Sun

Palace Theatre
A short walk north of the train station, the flatiron-shaped,
Grade II listed Palace Theatre – originally called 'The Pavilion' –
is one of only two purpose-built music halls left in the UK.
Stars who have trodden its 19th-century boards include Lillie
Langtry, Marie Lloyd, Morecambe and Wise, and Sir Anthony
Hopkins. The building is currently up for sale and a campaign
headed by actor Edward Fox has been launched to buy and
restore it. 🅐 top of High Street 🆆 www.pavrep.org
🆔 Bus: 120, 125

Wind Street

These days Wind (pronounced 'wine') Street is the place to head for an evening's partying but, as one of the main streets into Swansea since medieval times, it used to be better known as a place of commerce; Wales's first daily newspaper *The Cambrian* was founded here. It's one of the few areas of Swansea to have escaped bombing during World War II, so take a break from drinking to look up and admire the Flemish-style gabled rooftops. Check out the No Sign Bar, which is Swansea's oldest building after the Cross Keys.

CULTURE

Glynn Vivian Art Gallery

Founded by Richard Glynn Vivian, youngest son of local copper magnate John Henry Vivian, this impressive, neoclassical gallery

⬤ *The old gabled houses on Wind Street*

opened in 1911. Highlights include works by Claude Monet, Barbara Hepworth, the Welsh-born Rodin model, Gwen John, and the acclaimed local artist Ceri Richards. The gallery also has a significant collection of Swansea pottery. ➋ Alexandra Road ➊ 01792 516900 Ⓦ www.swansea.gov.uk/glynnvivian Ⓛ 10.00–17.00 Tues–Sun, closed Mon except bank holidays

Grand Theatre

Well-known comedians, touring plays and musicals, dance companies and mediums – they all come here. The **Arts Wing** hosts free art exhibitions as well as small-scale music and drama events, plus a monthly comedy club. The rooftop café-bar offers wonderful views across Swansea. ➋ Singleton Street ➊ 01792 475715 Ⓦ www.swansea.gov.uk/grandtheatre Ⓛ 09.30–18.00 daily (later on performance days)

St Mary's Church

There has been a church on this site since the 14th century but the current structure was built after World War II. Inside you'll find work by local artists, notably *The Deposition* by Ceri Richards,

SWANSEA POTTERY
In the 18th and 19th centuries, the Cambrian Pottery and Glamorgan Pottery were producing works to rival the best in the world. The Cambrian's business strategy was based on that of Josiah Wedgwood and many of its artists came from Staffordshire.

and stained glass made at the world-renowned Welsh School of Architectural Glass at Swansea's Metropolitan University. The church regularly hosts organ recitals and concerts.
ⓐ St Mary's Square ⓣ 01792 655489/298616 ⓦ www.swansea stmary.fsnet.co.uk

Ty Tawe

This little shop just off The Kingsway has been promoting the Welsh language and culture in Swansea for more than 20 years. As well as selling Welsh-language books and gifts, they also host Welsh classes and events to celebrate significant dates in the Welsh calendar, such as St David's Day (1 March). ⓐ 9 Christina Street ⓣ 01792 456856 ⓦ www.sioptytawe.co.uk ⓛ 09.30–14.00, 14.30–17.00 Mon–Fri, 10.00–14.00, 14.30–16.00 Sat, closed Sun

▲ *Swansea pottery on display in the Glynn Vivian Art Gallery*

RETAIL THERAPY

Most of the city centre's shops can be found on and around Oxford Street and in the Quadrant Shopping Centre. Here are some independent retailers that are well worth a browse. **Hobo's** vintage clothes rival Camden's finest. There's also a skate-wear shop, Exist, out the back. 📍 214 Oxford Street 📞 01792 654586 🌐 www.hobosswansea.co.uk 🕐 11.00–17.30 Mon–Sat, 12.00–16.00 Sun

Moda The place to go for men's and women's designer fashion: find Emporio Armani and Alexander McQueen, among others. There's also a smart but affordable café-bar. 📍 66–67 The Kingsway 📞 01792 469100 🌐 www.modacollections.co.uk 🕐 09.30–17.00 Mon–Sat, 11.00–16.00 Sun

Swansea Indoor Market Wales's largest indoor market has more than 100 stalls, selling everything from local produce to crystals. Highlights include welsh cakes from the Norfolk Bakery (stand C3), cockles and laverbread (CR1–6) and Goodie's (57A) for its

READ ALL ABOUT IT

To find out more about Swansea's history, read Nigel Jenkins' *Real Swansea* (Seren), *A Swansea Anthology* edited by James A Davies (Seren) and *Swansea's Heritage* by Richard Porch (The History Press). Also check out 🌐 www.swanseaheritage.net.

⬥ *Welsh woollens for sale in The Sheep Shop*

excellent selection of regional and European cheeses. ⓐ Oxford Street ⓣ 01792 654296 ⓦ www.swanseaindoormarket.co.uk ⓛ 08.00–17.30 Mon–Fri, 07.30–17.30 Sat, closed Sun

The Sheep Shop From fluffy sheep to Celtic crosses, you're sure to find something here to take home for friends and family. ⓐ 38–39 Castle Street ⓣ 01792 645718 ⓛ 09.30–17.30 Mon–Sat, closed Sun

TAKING A BREAK

CAFÉS
Govinda's £ ❶ It might seem unlikely to look at it, but this Hare Krishna-run café has regularly been voted one of the best vegetarian restaurants in Britain. Both veggies and carnivores head here for the good-value Indian food, fresh juices and vegan

cakes. ⓐ 8 Cradock Street ⓣ 01792 468469 ⓛ 12.00–15.00 Mon–Fri, 12.00–17.00 Sat

Holbrook's £ ❷ Set up by a former Swansea University student, this café is best known for its Fairtrade coffee and award-winning Gower Cottage chocolate brownies, but it also serves up tasty paninis and salads. ⓐ 28 Union Street ⓣ 01792 477797 ⓦ www.holbrooksonline.co.uk ⓛ 08.00–17.00 Mon–Sat, closed Sun

Kardomah £ ❸ This legendary Swansea café, which boasts 20 varieties of coffee beans, is very popular with older members of the community for its daily roast lunches. However, uniformed waitresses take orders from all ages. ⓐ 11 Portland Street ⓣ 01792 652336 ⓦ www.kardomahcoffeeshop.co.uk ⓛ 07.30–17.00 Mon–Sat, closed Sun

RESTAURANTS
If you only have a short time to spare, head to Wind Street where you can take your pick from several chain restaurants.

Wild Swan £–££ ❹ The pick of Swansea's Chinese restaurants. Have a drink at the bar and watch the Koi carp swim around before ordering some tasty Cantonese specialities. Service is fast and friendly and they do takeaways too. ⓐ 14–16 Orchard Street ⓣ 01792 472121 ⓛ 12.00–13.45, 18.00–23.30 daily

Bouchon de Rossi ££ ❺ A stylish little bistro opposite the Grand Theatre, which serves up grills, salads and baguettes at lunchtime and more sophisticated offerings in the evening, such as lemon sole and veal. The bavarois Grand Marnier is a recommended dessert. **@** 217 Oxford Street **@** 01792 655780 **@** www.bouchonderossi.co.uk **@** 12.00–14.00, 18.00–21.30 Tues–Sat, closed Sun

Dragon Brasserie ££ @ Arguably the best restaurant in the city centre, their European menu includes the likes of roasted streaky pork with Toulouse sausage on creamed Savoy cabbage followed by apple & pear crumble with butterscotch sauce. Good-value set lunch and dinner menus. **@** The Dragon Hotel, The Kingsway **@** 01792 657100 **@** www.dragon-hotel.co.uk **@** 12.00–14.30, 18.00–21.30 Mon–Thur & Sun, 12.00–14.30, 18.00–22.00 Fri & Sat

Mamma Mia ££ @ At this bright and lively Italian restaurant you can enjoy a risotto frutti di mare (prawns, red mullet, squid, parmesan) or a pizza misto di carne (ground beef, roast chicken, ham, spicy sausage) with your glass of Chianti. **@** 18–20 Princess Way **@** 01792 465465 **@** www.mymammamia.com **@** 12.00–15.00 & 18.00–22.00 Mon–Sat, 12.00–15.00 & 18.00–21.00 Sun

THE KARDOMAH GANG

In its original home on Castle Street (it was bombed during World War II), the Kardomah was a regular meeting place in the 1930s for Dylan Thomas, artist Alfred Janes, composer Daniel Jones and poet Vernon Watkins, who became known as 'The Kardomah Gang'.

La Braseria ££–£££ ❽ Buzzy Spanish restaurant. Pick your meat or fish at the counter and remember to save room for the profiteroles. No reservations (unless there's more than six of you), so be prepared to wait for a table at the weekend. ⓐ 28 Wind Street ⓣ 01792 469683 ⓛ 12.00–14.30, 19.00–23.00 Mon–Thur, 12.00–14.30, 19.00–23.30 Fri & Sat, closed Sun

Hanson at The Chelsea Café ££–£££ ❾ This is the place to go if you're a fish fan, but carnivores won't be disappointed. There's usually locally caught sea bass on the daily specials board. It is small, so book in advance. ⓐ 17 St Mary Street ⓣ 01792 464068 ⓛ 12.00–14.00, 19.00–21.30 Mon–Sat, 12.00–14.00 Sun

AFTER DARK

PUBS & BARS

Monkey Café ❿ Whatever you're into, you're sure to find something to please at Swansea's premier 'alternative' venue, whether you want to sip a cocktail, get down to some drum & bass, or catch a band. ⓐ 13 Castle Street ⓣ 01792 480822 ⓦ www.monkeycafe.co.uk ⓛ from 11.00 daily (closing times vary)

No Sign Bar ⓫ One of Swansea's best-known watering holes, the No Sign has been serving weary travellers since the 1600s. There's a good choice of ales, whiskies and wine, and now cocktails are on the menu too. The downstairs Vault has regular comedy and live music nights. And the food is pretty good – they make the best chips in town. ⓐ 56 Wind Street ⓣ 01792 456110 ⓛ 11.00–23.30 Mon–Thur, until 01.00 Sat, 12.00–23.30 Sun

Walkabout **12** You probably won't find many Antipodeans in here, but you'll encounter plenty of sports fans as this place shows all the major sporting events on big screens.
ⓐ 5–6 Castle Square ⓣ 01792 450850 ⓦ www.walkabout.eu.com
ⓛ from 12.00 daily (closing times vary)

CLUBS & VENUES

Milkwoodjam **13** Live music venue that showcases some of the world's best blues musicians but doesn't turn away other genres. It's 'open mic' night on Wednesdays. ⓐ 50 Plymouth Street ⓣ 01792 477577 ⓦ www.milkwoodjam.com

Oceana **14** Swansea's biggest and best nightclub, with five bars, ranging from the Parisian Boudoir to Tokyo, and three dance floors, including the New York Disco. Attracts top international DJs.
ⓐ 72 The Kingsway ⓣ 0845 293 2872 ⓦ www.oceanaclubs.com

Sin City **15** Part-run by Swansea University, this is the place for indie kids and metalheadz. There are DJ nights to suit most tastes as well as live bands and even a 'silent' disco. ⓐ Dillwyn Street ⓣ 01792 468892 ⓦ www.sincityclub.co.uk

CINEMAS

Odeon **16** Ten-screen cinema showing the latest blockbusters.
ⓐ Parc Tawe ⓣ 08712 244007 ⓦ www.odeon.co.uk

Vue **17** Twelve-screen cinema with special screenings for over 18s and a Ben & Jerry's counter. ⓐ York Street ⓣ 08712 240240
ⓦ www.myvue.com

The waterfront

On the south side of Oystermouth Road, a hop and a skip from the city centre, is Swansea's redeveloped docks area. This is where you'll find three of Swansea's museums, the LC (leisure centre), Wales's tallest building, a boating marina and, at the city's eastern approach, the new multimillion pound SA1 development. A promenade bordered by a long sandy beach runs from here all the way to Mumbles.

SIGHTS & ATTRACTIONS

Georgian Swansea

Prior to it becoming one of the drivers of Britain's Industrial Revolution, it was hoped that Swansea would rival Brighton and Bath as a fashionable resort. The city's Georgian past is still

DOCTOR WHO

Swansea has featured in several episodes of *Doctor Who* since the series came back on to our screens in 2005. In the Christmas-set episode, 'The Unquiet Dead', Cambrian Place was transformed into a snowy Victorian street, while in the third Christmas Special, 'Voyage of the Damned', Kylie Minogue came to town to film inside the Exchange Buildings on the corner of Adelaide Street. The man responsible for *Doctor Who*'s successful relaunch, Russell T Davies, was born in the city.

visible in the architecture of Gloucester Place, Somerset Place and Cambrian Place; the latter is the location of the Assembly Rooms, which were built in 1821 as a place of entertainment for 'polite society' and have now been converted into flats.

The Maritime Quarter

In the 1980s the old South Dock was transformed into an award-winning Blue Flag marina surrounded by low-rise apartment blocks. That all changed in 2009, when the 29-storey Meridian Tower apartment highrise was completed, making it the tallest building in Wales at 90 m (295 ft) high.

Morgans Hotel

Now the city's swishest hotel, the impressive Grade-II-listed red-brick building east of Swansea Museum opened its doors in 1903 as the HQ of Swansea Harbour Trust. The building was designed by a Cardiff architect, Edwin Seward, whose company also designed Cardiff's Coal Exchange and Free Library.

ⓐ Somerset Place, Maritime Quarter ⓘ 01792 484848
ⓦ www.morganshotel.co.uk

SA1

At the eastern entrance to the city, SA1 is Swansea's latest residential, business and leisure development around the old Prince of Wales Dock. Buildings of note include the **Norwegian Church**, a onetime place of worship for Norwegian sailors; the **J-Shed** – a 19th-century grain warehouse; and **The Ice House**, a 19th-century ice-making factory for the local fishing industry. The area is linked to the Maritime Quarter by the Sail Bridge.

◓ *Looking towards Swansea across Swansea Bay*

Sail Bridge

At 140 m (460 ft) long and with a mast 40 m (130 ft) high, the award-winning Sail Bridge crosses the River Tawe to link the new SA1 development with the Maritime Quarter and city centre.

Swansea Observatory

At the eastern end of the Promenade, behind the marina, is a building that looks like a rocket waiting to be launched. This is Swansea Observatory, also known as the Tower of the Ecliptic, and was occupied by the Swansea Astronomical Society from its opening in 1993 until 2010. Unfortunately, the structure is currently closed to the public, which means that visitors can't enjoy the stained-glass roof flooding coloured light on to the spiral staircase.

CULTURE

Dylan Thomas Centre

The grand façade of Swansea's 19th-century town hall now houses the world's largest collection of Dylan Thomas memorabilia. Highlights of the fascinating multi-media exhibition include the original garage doors from his 'writing shed' in Laugharne, costumes from the 2008 film, *The Edge of Love*, and his entry for the first Surrealist exhibition in London in 1936. The centre hosts the annual Dylan Thomas Festival at the end of October but puts on literary events throughout the year. Be sure to check out the specialist bookshop before leaving.

ⓐ Somerset Place, Maritime Quarter ☏ 01792 463980
Ⓦ www.dylanthomas.com ⏱ 10.00–16.30 daily

Dylan Thomas Theatre

Instantly recognisable by its *trompe l'oeil* murals, this terracotta-coloured building has been home to Swansea Little Theatre since the 1980s. It is named after the writer as he was a member of the theatre group in the 1930s, and the current troupe regularly puts on productions of his plays. In the square in front of the theatre there is a bronze statue, by John Doubleday, of Dylan sitting on a chair. ⓐ Gloucester Place, Maritime Quarter ⓣ 01792 473238 ⓦ www.dylanthomas theatre.org.uk

National Waterfront Museum

The latest addition to Swansea's collection of museums charts the industrial history of Wales since the 18th century. Here you'll find out what life was like in Swansea in the 1850s, the inventions that Wales gave to the world and the contributions the country continues to make in the fields of medicine, science and technology. There are regular exhibitions and a pleasant open-plan café. ⓐ Oystermouth Road ⓣ 01792 638950 ⓦ www.museumwales.ac.uk/swansea ⓛ 10.00–17.00 daily

LITERARY LOLLY

The Dylan Thomas Prize is the world's largest literary prize for writers aged under 30. It was launched in 2006 and awards £30,000 to the winning author each year. ⓦ www.thedylanthomasprize.com

Swansea Museum

Dylan Thomas described Swansea Museum as a 'museum that should be in a museum', and it's not difficult to see why; it is, after all, Wales's oldest museum. Inside its imposing 1840s neoclassical façade you'll find a 'cabinet of curiosities', an Egyptian mummy and a collection of Swansea Pottery, but the most interesting display is of local archaeology. It also has a 'floating collection' of boats in the marina and some carriages from Mumbles Train (see page 74).

ⓐ Oystermouth Road ⓣ 01792 653763 ⓦ www.swansea.gov.uk/swanseamuseum ⓛ 10.00–17.00 Tues–Sun, closed Mon except bank holidays

🔺 *The Dylan Thomas Centre*

RETAIL THERAPY

There are few shops in this area other than chandlers and a supermarket, but here are three that are worth a look:

The Environment Centre This centre has a shop with Fairtrade food and gifts as well as information on environmental issues. ⓐ The Old Telephone Exchange, Pier Street ⓣ 01792 480200 ⓦ www.environmentcentre.org.uk ⓛ 10.00–16.00 Mon–Fri, closed Sat & Sun

Nick Holly Gallery Art gallery showing some of Swansea's most accomplished artists. ⓐ Exchange Building, Cambrian Place, Maritime Quarter ⓣ 01792 483962 ⓦ www.nickholly.com ⓛ 10.00–17.00 Wed–Sat, 11.00–16.00 Sun, closed Mon & Tues

Palterman & Thomas @ The Norwegian Church Lovely collection of contemporary jewellery by Welsh and international designers. The owners take commissions and are particularly noted for their rings. There's also a small exhibition on the history of the building. ⓐ Norwegian Church, Langdon Road ⓣ 01792 641441 ⓦ www.paltermanandthomas.com ⓛ 10.00–17.00 Tues–Sat, closed Sun & Mon ⓝ Bus: 44, 156

TAKING A BREAK

CAFÉS
Café Two-Cann £ ⓲ Situated in a historic former grain warehouse, this sophisticated gastro café serves its delicious

🔺 *The historic J-Shed now houses cafés and restaurants*

coffees with mini Welsh cakes. Relax in a leather armchair and munch on a club sandwich for lunch, or come on a Friday or Saturday for dinner. ⓐ Unit 2, J-Shed, King's Road ① 01792 458000 ⓦ www.cafetwocann.com ⓒ 11.00–16.00 Mon–Fri, 10.00–16.00 Sat & Sun, 17.30–19.45 Fri & Sat ⓝ Bus: 44, 156

Fresco £ ⑲ This bright, modern café overlooking the marina is the place to come for home-made Italian ice creams and sorbets. On colder days a coffee or a hot chocolate will revive you. ⓐ Unit 2, National Waterfront Museum, Oystermouth Road ① 01792 472331 ⓒ 10.00–18.00 daily (closing times vary in winter)

The Ice House £ ⑳ An old docks warehouse that has been transformed into a glass-fronted café and art gallery. There's a good choice of snacks, and it's licensed too. There's usually live music or comedy at the weekend. ⓐ King's Road ⓣ 01792 649060 ⓦ www.theicehouseswansea.co.uk ⓛ 08.30–22.00 Mon, until 18.00 Tues, until 23.00 Wed–Sat, 09.00–22.00 Sun ⓝ Bus: 44, 156

RESTAURANTS

The Thai Elephant £–££ ㉑ This authentic Thai restaurant is instantly recognisable by the two pachyderms either side of the door. The hot hot Thai green curry and nutty Pad Thai come recommended. ⓐ The Ice House, King's Road ⓣ 01792 650050 ⓦ www.thaielephantswansea.com ⓛ 12.00–14.30, 18.00–23.00 daily ⓝ Bus: 44, 156

Charlie's ££ ㉒ Cosy basement restaurant in a Georgian terrace opposite Morgans Hotel. The menu is weighted towards local specialities such as cockles and laverbread, and Glamorgan sausages. The upstairs cocktail bar is a popular place to kick off the evening. ⓐ 2 Prospect Place, Maritime Quarter ⓣ 01792 413290 ⓦ www.charliesdining.co.uk ⓛ 12.00–14.30 Wed–Sun, 18.00–21.30 Wed–Sat, closed Sun eve, Mon & Tues

Gallini's ££ ㉓ Overlooking the marina, this highly regarded restaurant has been serving up fish and Italian food for more than ten years. Lunch can be a simple affair with sandwiches and salads but lobster, duck and venison feature in the evening. ⓐ Unit 3, Fishmarket Quay, Maritime Quarter ⓣ 01792 456285 ⓦ www.gallinisrestaurant.co.uk ⓛ 12.00–14.30, 18.00–21.30 Mon–Sat, closed Sun

La Parrilla ££–£££ ㉔ The younger, more sophisticated sister of La Braseria has become one of the city's most fashionable eateries. Boasting the largest selection of seafood on offer in Swansea and a wine menu that includes Château Petrus, this is the place to go to impress. However, you can also get a two-course lunch for less than a tenner. ⓐ J-Shed, King's Road ⓣ 01792 464530 ⓦ www.laparrilla.co.uk ⓛ 12.00–14.30, 19.00–22.30 Tues–Thur; 12.00–14.30, 18.30–22.30 Fri & Sat, 12.00–16.00 Sun, closed Sun eve & Mon ⓝ Bus: 44, 156

AFTER DARK

Morgans Bar ㉕ Sink into a leather sofa and quaff some champagne or a cocktail in the cavernous, and sometimes draughty, bar of this grand listed building. Don't expect service with a smile and do expect to fork out. ⓐ Morgans Hotel, Somerset Place, Maritime Quarter ⓣ 01792 484848 ⓦ www.morganshotel.co.uk ⓛ 11.00–23.00 Mon–Thur, 11.00–01.00 Fri & Sat, 11.00–22.30 Sun

The Queen's ㉖ Once the place where sailors went to pick up prostitutes (they used to put the price on the soles of their shoes), this old docks pub still retains its 19th-century charm but now attracts journalists from the nearby *South Wales Evening Post*, academics, fishermen and everyone in between. Most come to sample the real ales on offer but others come for the home-cooked food; there's live music on Saturday nights. ⓐ Gloucester Place, Maritime Quarter ⓣ 01792 521531 ⓛ 11.00–23.00 Mon–Fri, 11.00–23.30 Sat, 12.00–22.30 Sun

Swansea West

Once the domain of wealthy 19th-century industrialists, the west of Swansea is now home to many of the thousands of students who study in the city. Both Uplands, the birthplace of Dylan Thomas, and Brynmill are dotted with quirky cafés, pubs, restaurants and shops, especially along Bryn-y-Mor Road and Uplands Crescent; there's a cluster of excellent live music venues here too. Leading out of the city centre, St Helen's Road is where you'll find the city's best Indian restaurants and ethnic foodshops. The west is also home to the city's main parks and university.

SIGHTS & ATTRACTIONS

Clyne Gardens

Situated between the university and Mumbles, Clyne Gardens was once an estate owned by the Vivian family, Swansea's 19th-century copper magnates. As well as an attractive bluebell wood, a wildflower meadow and heather beds, the park has an internationally important collection of rhododendrons and is home to the tallest recorded magnolia in Britain. The 'Clyne in Bloom' festival celebrates the park in all its glory in May.

ⓐ Mumbles Road (next to The Woodman pub) ☏ 01792 401737 ⓦ www.swansea.gov.uk/parks Ⓥ Bus: 2, 2A, 2B, 2C, 3, 3A

Constitution Hill

One of Swansea's most unforgettable sights is this cobbled hill, the city's steepest residential area, with a gradient of up to 30 per cent; it was made famous as the location of a car chase in the 1997 film *Twin Town* starring Rhys Ifans and Dougray Scott. More recently it has been part of the route for the poor riders in the Tour of Britain cycle race. ⓐ off Walter Road

Cwmdonkin Park

This park in the heart of Uplands is a 'must visit' for fans of Dylan Thomas, as he was born nearby at Cwmdonkin Drive (*No 5*), where he wrote much of his poetry. The park inspired and featured in some of his work, notably 'The Hunchback in the Park'. A rock inscribed with the final lines from 'Fern Hill' commemorates him. There are some lovely woodland walks and a children's play area. ⓐ Park Drive, Uplands
ⓦ www.swansea.gov.uk/parks ⓝ Bus: 20, 20A, 21, 22, 37

◭ *It's a long climb to the top of Constitution Hill*

DYLAN THOMAS

Dylan Marlais Thomas was born in Uplands on 27 October 1914 and went on to become one of the greatest poets of the 20th century. After a couple of years spent as a reporter on the *South Wales Daily Post*, he moved to London then back to Wales, to Laugharne in Carmarthenshire, to focus on his writing. His best-known work is probably the radio play *Under Milk Wood*, which was turned into a film starring Richard Burton and Elizabeth Taylor. Dylan died in New York on 9 November 1953 during a literary tour. ⓦ www.dylanthomas.com

Singleton Park

Next to the university, Swansea's largest park was another of the Vivian family's estates. As well as plenty of green space, the Botanical Gardens have a highly regarded collection of plants from around the world, which are best admired during August's 'Botanics in Bloom' festival. There's a boating lake with ducks and geese to amuse kids and The Pub on the Pond for thirsty adults. ⓐ Oystermouth Road ⓣ 01792 297854 ⓦ www.swansea.gov.uk/parks ⓝ Bus: 2, 2A, 2B, 2C, 3, 3A

CULTURE

The Brangwyn Hall & Guildhall

This grand space in Swansea's Guildhall is the city's premier venue for classical music concerts. The hall is named after Sir

⬥ *The house where Dylan Thomas was born*

Frank Brangwyn, whose 17 colourful British Empire Panels, originally destined for the House of Lords, now grace the walls of the auditorium; they can be visited during the Guildhall's opening hours. ⓐ South Road ⓣ 01792 635432 ⓦ www.swansea.gov.uk/brangwynhall ⓛ 08.30–16.30 Mon–Fri, closed Sat & Sun and during private functions ⓝ Bus: 2, 2A, 2B, 2C, 3, 3A

Taliesin Arts Centre
This arts centre on the university campus is home to a theatre, which showcases experimental drama, arthouse cinema, dance and world music, and the Ceri Richards Gallery, named after the highly acclaimed local artist, which hosts regular exhibitions by national and international artists. Also in the building is The Egypt Centre, a museum of Egyptian artefacts. ⓐ University campus ⓣ 01792 602060 (box office), 01792 295526, (gallery), 01792 295960 (Egypt Centre) ⓦ www.taliesinartscentre.co.uk ⓛ Box office & gallery: 10.00–18.00 Mon–Fri, 10.00–13.00, 13.30–16.00 Sat, closed Sun; Egypt Centre: 10.00–16.00 Tues–Sat, closed Sun & Mon ⓝ Bus: 2, 2A, 2B, 2C, 3, 3A

DID YOU KNOW?
Apart from Dylan Thomas, other famous residents of Uplands included writer Sir Kingsley Amis, who lived in The Grove when he taught at the university from 1949 to 1961, and former Conservative Deputy Prime Minister Michael Heseltine, who was born and brought up in Eaton Crescent.

RETAIL THERAPY

Crundles An Aladdin's Cave of chunky jewellery made with semi-precious stones plus a colourful range of ethnic clothes and home furnishings from around the world. 🅰 80 Bryn-y-Mor Road ☎ 01792 462585 🆆 www.crundles.com 🕘 09.30–17.00 Mon–Sat, closed Sun 🚌 Bus: 2, 2A, 2B, 2C, 3, 3A

Uplands Bookshop Although it sells books of all genres, this bookshop is best known for its maps, travel guidebooks and children's literature. 🅰 27 Uplands Crescent ☎ 01792 470195 🕘 09.00–17.30 Mon–Sat, closed Sun 🚌 Bus: 20, 20A, 21, 22, 37

TAKING A BREAK

CAFÉS

Joe's £ ㉗ This ice-cream parlour is renowned for its creamy vanilla-flavoured ice cream; try it in a cherry temptation sundae. They also have outlets at Newton Road in Mumbles and The Piazza in Parc Tawe. 🅰 85 St Helen's Road ☎ 01792 653880 🆆 www.joes-icecream.com 🕘 11.00–21.00 Mon–Fri, 12.00–20.00 Sat & Sun 🚌 Bus: 2, 2A, 2B, 2C, 3, 3A

One Shoe Café £ ㉘ This is a tiny café next to Truffle restaurant where students and workers flock for the home-made chocolate brownies. On fine days, munch a baguette or panini at one of their pavement tables. 🅰 1 King Edward Road ☎ 07543 439595 🕘 08.30–16.30 Mon–Fri, closed Sat & Sun 🚌 Bus: 2, 2A, 2B, 2C, 3, 3A

The Shed £ ㉙ Admire the artworks by local artists as you sip a smoothie or quaff a coffee in this gallery-cum-coffeeshop. The exhibitions change every Sunday. ⓐ 47 Uplands Crescent ⓣ 01792 516763 ⓦ www.shedgallery.com ⓛ 09.00–18.00 Mon–Fri, 10.00–18.00 Sat, closed Sun ⓝ Bus: 20, 20A, 21, 22, 37

RESTAURANTS

Truffle £ ㉚ Popular restaurant with a penchant for Eastern flavours – try slow-cooked lamb tagine with couscous – although there are favourites like steak and chips too. Bring your own bottle as there's no corkage charge. ⓐ 68 Bryn-y-Mor Road ⓣ 01792 547246 ⓦ www.truffle-swansea.co.uk ⓛ 18.30–23.00 Wed–Sat, closed Sun–Tues ⓝ Bus: 2, 2A, 2B, 2C, 3, 3A

The Viceroy of India £ ㉛ It's unlikely you'll be disappointed with any of the Indian restaurants along St Helen's Road, but this one is a long-standing favourite with locals. House specialities include Goan roast duckling and trout tandoori, which are best washed down with a Kingfisher beer. ⓐ 50 St Helen's Road ⓣ 01792 466898 ⓦ www.viceroyswansea.co.uk ⓛ 17.30–01.00 Sun–Thur, 17.30–03.00 Fri & Sat ⓝ Bus: 2, 2A, 2B, 2C, 3, 3A

Wasabi £ ㉜ This might not look much from the outside, but inside is some of the best Japanese food you'll taste anywhere. If sushi and sashimi aren't your kettle of fish, opt for some Yaki Soba or Udon noodles accompanied by assorted tempura. They also do take-aways. ⓐ 49 Uplands Crescent ⓣ 01792 464999 ⓛ 12.00–14.30 & 17.30–23.00 Mon–Thur, 12.00–23.00 Fri & Sat, 12.00–22.30 Sun & bank holidays ⓝ Bus: 20, 20A, 21, 22, 37

Pant-y-Gwydr ££–£££ ㉝ It's worth seeking out this recently opened French restaurant for its authentic bistro staples such as cassoulet, steak frites and pot au feu; the Parisian chef makes his own fresh-fruit sorbets. Come in for a coffee and a cake in between meals. ⓐ corner of Oxford Street and Richardson Street ⓣ 01792 455498 ⓛ 12.00–14.15 & 18.00–22.15, closed Sun & Mon

Slice ££–£££ ㉞ The owners of this first-floor restaurant have worked in the kitchens of some of Britain's best-known chefs and now use their skills transforming local produce into tasty dishes with a Mediterranean twist – like Gower asparagus with Parmesan shavings followed by roast saddle of lamb with rosemary polenta. ⓐ 73–75 Eversley Road, Sketty ⓣ 01792 290929 ⓦ www.sliceswansea.co.uk ⓛ 12.00–14.00 & 18.30–21.00 Thur–Sun, closed Mon–Wed ⓝ Bus: 20, 20A, 21, 22, 37

AFTER DARK

PUBS

Uplands Tavern ㉟ Once a favourite watering hole of Dylan Thomas, this pub has long been a stalwart of Swansea's live music scene. On most nights, local and touring bands play rock, blues and pop. There's a pleasant flower-bedecked terrace for sunny days. ⓐ 42 Uplands Crescent ⓣ 01792 458242 ⓦ www.myspace.com/uplandstavern ⓛ 12.00–23.00 Sun–Thur, 12.00–24.00 Fri & Sat ⓝ Bus: 20, 20A, 21, 22, 37

The Westbourne ㊱ This smart, independently run pub has four large screens to entertain sports fans, while connoisseurs of real ale won't be disappointed. ⓐ 1 Bryn-y-Mor Road ⓣ 01792 476637 ⓦ www.westbourneswansea.com ⓛ 12.00–23.00 Sun & Mon, 12.00–23.30 Tues & Wed, 12.00–24.00 Thur, 12.00–00.30 Fri & Sat ⓝ Bus: 2, 2A, 2B, 2C, 3, 3A

VENUES

The Chattery ㊲ This café is best known for its live music on weekend nights. It's a favourite with an older crowd who come to listen to singer-songwriters and 'alternative country' bands. ⓐ 59 Uplands Crescent ⓣ 01792 473276 ⓦ http://homepage. ntlworld.com/thechattery ⓛ 10.00–17.00 (16.30 on music nights); open from 19.30 for music ⓝ Bus: 20, 20A, 21, 22, 37

The Garage ㊳ Live bands and DJs of a variety of genres, as well as comedy nights, are on the agenda at this venue. ⓐ 47 Uplands Crescent ⓣ 01792 475147 ⓦ www.garagevenue.com ⓝ Bus: 20, 20A, 21, 22, 37

Swansea Jazzland ㊴ Some of the world's best jazz musicians head here to give memorable concerts. Their 'Sunday Jazz Lunch' is always popular; they also hold masterclasses and workshops. ⓐ St James Social Club, St James Crescent, Uplands ⓣ 01792 380615 ⓦ www.swanseajazzland.co.uk ⓝ Bus: 20, 20A, 21, 22, 37

▶ *Mumbles as seen from Swansea Bay*

OUT OF TOWN
trips

Mumbles

This former oyster-fishing village is now best known as the place where Hollywood actress Catherine Zeta-Jones grew up; her family still lives here. The fishing boats have long gone, replaced with weekend dinghies and catamarans, and Mumbles is now the area's most desirable location to live and play. Explore the boutiques of Newton Road before stepping back in time past the fishermen's cottages of Village Lane; then take a walk along the front and pause to think about the much-missed Mumbles Train, the world's first passenger train service, which ferried people from Swansea to Mumbles from 1806 to 1960.

To get here these days, take the No 3 bus – it's a 15-minute journey; or if you're with kids, get off at Blackpill and hop on the Swansea Bay Rider (☎ 01792 635411 ⓦ www.swanseaprom.com), the bright red 'land train', which runs along the Prom. Drop by the well-stocked Tourist Information Centre (ⓐ Methodist Church, 522 Mumbles Road ☎ 01792 361302

COASTAL CAPER

Explore the Gower coast in a high-speed yellow RIB – 'Sea Serpent' – with Gower Coast Adventures. Along the way you'll encounter some of Britain's best beaches, historic caves and marine wildlife – you might even see dolphins and porpoises on the three-hour trip to Worm's Head.
ⓐ Knab Rock (by Verdi's) ☎ 07866 250440
ⓦ www.gowercoastadventures.co.uk ☻ Easter–Sept

ⓦ www.visitmumbles.co.uk) to find out more about Mumbles and Gower.

SIGHTS & ATTRACTIONS

Mumbles Hill Nature Reserve

Once used for common grazing and limestone quarrying, Mumbles Hill is now protected for its maritime heath and limestone scrub, grassland and woodland. Remnants of anti-aircraft guns and bunkers from World War II can still be seen. The views over the South Wales and Somerset coasts are magnificent. ⓐ Access for all from Thistleboon Drive, other footpaths at Dickslade and Bracelet Bay ⓣ 01792 635708 (for details of an all-ability access trail and audio guide) ⓦ www.swansea.gov.uk/mumbleshill

Mumbles Lighthouse

The unmanned solar-powered lighthouse dates from 1794. The stone buildings around it are military and were constructed in the 1860s. ⓐ Mumbles Head

Mumbles Pier

This Victorian pier used to be where visitors were unloaded from paddle steamers on to the Mumbles Train, but these days it's the place for a stroll followed by a coffee in the café or a pint in the pub. There's an amusement arcade complete with video games and ten-pin bowling. Controversial plans are afoot to turn the site into a hotel and leisure complex. ⓐ West end of the Promenade ⓣ 01792 365220 ⓦ www.mumbles-pier.co.uk

Oystermouth Castle

This 13th-century ruined castle has undergone a £1 million restoration, thanks to a grant from the Welsh government to make the site more accessible. You can walk around the grounds for free and they hold open-air productions of Shakespeare's plays here in summer. ⓐ Castle Avenue, off Newton Road ⓣ 01792 468321 ⓦ www.swansea.gov.uk/oystermouthcastle ⓛ 11.00–17.00 daily (Easter–Aug) ⓘ Admission charge

RETAIL THERAPY

Local Produce Market Popular farmers' market held on the second Saturday of every month, which showcases a wide variety of home-made goodies from lavender cupcakes to wild boar burgers. ⓐ The Dairy Car Park, Oystermouth Square ⓛ 09.00–13.00 second Sat of the month

The Lovespoon Gallery Lovespoons are carved wooden spoons that have been given as tokens of affection in Wales since the 16th century. They are popular wedding gifts and this shop sells works by Wales's top carvers. ⓐ 492 Mumbles Road ⓣ 01792 360132 ⓦ www.thelovespoongallery.com ⓛ 10.00–17.30 Mon–Sat, closed Sun

Oyster Gallery Stylish gifts from sea-inspired home decoration to lovely local views by Swansea-based artists and photographers. Stunning silver jewellery by Gower-based designer Pa-pa (ⓦ www.pa-pa.co.uk). ⓐ 70–72 Newton Road ⓣ 01792 366988 ⓦ www.oystergallery.co.uk ⓛ 09.00–17.30 Mon–Sat, 11.00–16.00 Sun

⚫ *See an open-air Shakespeare performance at Oystermouth Castle*

TAKING A BREAK

CAFÉS

Café Valance £ Stylish café-bar where 'yummy mummies' come to sip a cappuccino or to chew the fat over a locally sourced burger. ⓐ 50 Newton Road ⓣ 01792 367711 ⓦ www. cafevalance.com ⓛ 08.30–23.00 Mon–Sat, 10.00–17.00 Sun

The Kitchen Table £ Catering for those who like their food and drink locally sourced, vegetarian or organic. Try a vegebree (veggie kedgeree), an organic Welsh Black beef pie or simply a tea or coffee. ⓐ 626 Mumbles Road ⓣ 01792 367616 ⓛ 09.00–17.30 Tues & Wed, until 21.30 Thur–Sun, closed Mon

Verdi's £ Sit on the terrace and lick one of the 30 flavours of ice cream or relax inside and admire the view. The pizza, pasta and focaccia sandwiches are recommended. ⓐ Knab Rock ⓣ 01792 369135 ⓦ www.verdis-cafe.co.uk ⓛ 10.00–21.30 daily (June–Sept until 22.00 during school summer holidays); 10.00–18.00 Mon–Thur, 10.00–21.00 Fri–Sun (Nov–Mar); 10.00–21.00 daily (Apr, May & Oct)

RESTAURANTS

Langland Brasserie £–£££ French, Italian and Welsh influences are evident at this lovely beachside restaurant about a mile from the centre of Mumbles where you can watch the surfers riding the waves. ⓐ Brynfield Road, Langland ⓣ 01792 363699 ⓦ www.langlandbrasserie.co.uk ⓛ 10.00–23.00 Mon–Thur, 10.00–23.30 Fri & Sat, 10.00–20.30 Sun ⓝ Bus: 2, 2A, 2B, 2C

🔺 *Lovespoons on display in The Lovespoon Gallery*

Norton House Hotel ££ Veteran chef Chris Keenan has long championed Gower's local produce, so you won't be surprised to find the likes of Welsh Rarebit with cockles, laverbread and bacon on the menu, which generally has a French flavour. The traditional Georgian surroundings are a great place for Sunday lunch. @ Norton Road ☏ 01792 404891 ⓦ www. nortonhousehotel.co.uk ⏱ 12.30–14.30 & 18.30–21.30 daily

PA's ££–£££ This award-winning eaterie has also been voted Swansea's best restaurant by readers of the local newspaper. Fish features prominently, with the likes of roast sea bass with king prawns in spring onion and ginger sauce, but there's something for everyone. An open fire warms in winter; opt for the garden on sunny days. @ 95 Newton Road ☏ 01792 367723 ⓦ www.paswinebar.co.uk ⏱ 12.00–14.30 & 19.00–21.30 Mon–Fri, 12.00–14.30 & 18.00–21.30 Sat, 12.00–14.30 Sun, closed Sun eve

AFTER DARK

Surf Club Small nightclub with urban, house and chart nights plus a special 'cabaret disco' for the over-30s. @ Castleton Walk, 26 Newton Road ☏ 01792 363650 ⓦ www.surfclubmumbles.co.uk ⏱ Wed–Sun (times vary)

The White Rose Offering cheap and cheerful drinks and food, this half-timbered pub has entertainment every night, from quizzes to karaoke. There's a courtyard terrace for sunny days. @ Bottom of Newton Road ☏ 01792 368426 ⏱ 09.30–23.00 Mon & Tues, 09.30–23.30 Wed & Thu, 09.30–24.00 Fri & Sat, 10.00–23.00 Sun

The Gower Peninsula

Jutting out into the sea for 26 km (16 miles) west of Swansea, the Gower Peninsula is one of the country's most popular tourist destinations. The area has been inhabited since Neolithic times – see some of the finds at Swansea Museum – but its charms were only officially recognised in 1956 when the peninsula became Britain's first Area of Outstanding Natural Beauty.

Gower is a 'must visit' for fans of watersports; surfers from around the world have been catching waves here for more than 40 years. These days there's also paddle-boarding and boogie-boarding for less energetic sorts, as well as a wide variety of other water- and land-based activities. Not to mention around 50 beaches, some of which have either Blue Flags or Green Coast Awards for cleanliness and environmental excellence.

The peninsula is best explored on foot or by bike. If you don't want to discover its coast, prehistoric monuments and villages alone, come for the **Gower Walking Festival** in June or the **Gower Cycling Festival** in September. The churches come to life in July when classical music concerts are held in some of the area's most attractive and historic places of worship (ⓦ www.gowerfestival.org). And if that isn't enough to keep you occupied, there are also many nature reserves and five castles. For general information on the area contact Mumbles Tourist Information Centre ⓐ Mumbles Methodist Church, 522 Mumbles Road ⓣ 01792 361302 ⓦ www.visitmumbles.co.uk ⓛ 10.00–17.00 Mon–Sat, 12.00–16.00 Sun (July & Aug); 10.00–16.00 Mon–Sat, closed Sun (Sept–June)

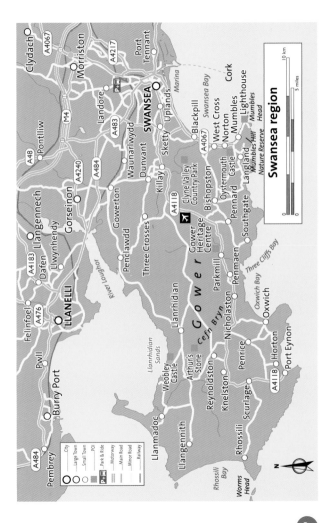

Swansea region

SIGHTS & ATTRACTIONS

Cefn Bryn

Known as the backbone of Gower, this 8-km (5-mile)-long ridge is popular with walkers and affords wonderful views over the coast from its highest point. The area is dotted with Neolithic monuments, the most famous of which is Arthur's Stone, a burial chamber. The walk is one of several inland and coastal routes on Gower. Hardy sorts should try The Gower Way (Ⓦ www.visitswanseabay.com/thegowerway), which stretches for 56 km (35 miles) from Gowerton in the north to Rhossili. Ⓐ Cilibion Ⓝ Bus: 115, 118

Llangennith

At the north end of Rhossili Bay, 'Gennith is a mecca for surfers of all abilities. However, the village has some historic interest too – the 12th-century church, **St Cenydd's**, is Gower's largest and **Burry Holms**, the small island off the beach, has remains of an Iron Age earthwork and a medieval monastery (note that it's only accessible for a couple of hours at low tide). Ⓝ Bus: 115,116

Rhossili & Worms Head

The best-known and most picturesque part of Gower was voted both Britain's best beach and picnic spot in 2010 by the British Guild of Travel Writers. Start your visit at the National Trust Visitor Centre and Shop (Ⓣ 01792 390707 Ⓦ www.nationaltrust.org.uk), where you can pick up a leaflet of local walks and find out if it's safe to explore the worm (Viking for 'dragon') – it gets cut off at high tide. The bits of wood sticking out of the sand

belong to *The Helvetia*, a Norwegian boat, which sank in 1887.
Bus: 118, X18

Three Cliffs Bay
This isn't the easiest beach to get to – past a ruined castle and
sometimes through a herd of cows – but it's one of Britain's
loveliest. At low tide you can walk through an arch in the cliffs
but it's generally best to avoid swimming, as the currents are
very strong here. ⓐ Southgate, Pennard ⓝ Bus: 14, 14A

Weobley Castle
Built by one of the lords of Gower in the 14th century, this castle
is in a dramatic position overlooking the Burry Estuary; inside is
an exhibition on the house and Gower. The area is best known
for its saltmarsh lamb, reared on the nearby Weobley Castle

▲ *Weobley Castle dates from the 14th century*

Farm (01792 391421 www.gowersaltmarshlamb.co.uk).
ⓐ Llanrhidian ☎ 01792 390012 ⓦ www.cadw.wales.gov.uk
🕒 09.30–18.00 daily (Apr–Oct); 09.30–17.00 daily (Nov–Mar)
Ⓝ Bus: 115, 116 ❶ Admission charge

CULTURE

Gower Heritage Centre

This rural life museum based around a 12th-century corn mill
has something for everyone: there are small animals, a tea room
serving cream teas and snacks made with local produce, as well
as a year-round events calendar, including the Gower Rock
Festival in July. Check out the craft shop for locally made
garden furniture. ⓐ Parkmill ☎ 01792 371206 ⓦ www.
gowerheritagecentre. co.uk 🕒 10.00–17.00 daily Ⓝ Bus: 117, 118,
X18 ❶ Admission charge (half price with Gower Explorer ticket)

TRAVEL GREEN

It's easier than ever to explore Gower without a car. Veolia
operates the Gower Explorer (Ⓝ Bus: 115, 116, 117, 118) from
Monday to Saturday to Oxwich, Port Eynon, Llangennith
and Rhossili; ask for a Gower Day Explorer ticket for
unlimited travel. First Cymru runs the 14 and 14A to
Pennard Cliffs from Monday to Saturday and the X18 to
Oxwich, Port Eynon and Rhossili on Saturdays and Sundays.
Baytrans (☎ 01792 205071 ⓦ www.baytrans.org.uk) has
information on buses and walks on Gower.

● Arthur's Stone is a Neolithic burial chamber

GET ACTIVE

Here's the pick of the activities available on Gower:

Bushcraft Discover how to survive in the wilds of Gower with **Dryad Bushcraft**; you can even become a 'castaway' or a 'wilderness gourmet'. ☎ 01792 547213 or 07901 873343 ⓦ www.dryadbushcraft.co.uk

Golf Voted one of the Top 60 golf courses in the UK, **Pennard Golf Club's** 18-hole course overlooks Three Cliffs Bay. ⓐ Southgate, Pennard ☎ 01792 233131 ⓦ www.pennardgolfclub.com Ⓝ Bus: 14, 14A

Horseriding See the Gower coast from the back of a horse with **Parc Le Breos**; a full day includes a scenic lunch stop. ⓐ Parkmill ☎ 01792 371636 ⓦ www.parc-le-breos.co.uk Ⓝ Bus: 117, 118, X18

Mountain boarding Learn cross-country skateboarding at the **Mountain Boarding Centre** in the grounds of Weobley Castle. ⓐ Llanrhidian ☎ 07856 152540 ⓦ www.brdsports. co.uk Ⓝ Bus: 115, 116

Surfing The **Welsh Surfing Federation School** is a non-profit-making school specialising in teaching beginners of all ages. ⓐ Hillend Campsite, Llangennith ☎ 01792 386426 ⓦ www.wsfsurfschool.co.uk Ⓝ Bus: 115, 116

RETAIL THERAPY

Gower Wildflower & Local Produce Centre The peninsula is well known for its biodiversity, and here you can buy a wide range of native plants, flowers, herbs and vegetables. The shop also stocks a good selection of local gastronomic favourites, such as cockles, saltmarsh lamb and jams. ❸ Blackhills Lane, Fairwood ❶ 01792 298496 ⓦ www.gowerwildflowers.co.uk ❶ 10.00–17.30 daily (times vary in winter)

PJ's Surf Shop Gen up on the local surf scene here and get kitted out. It's owned by former Welsh, British and European surf champion Pete Jones. ❸ Llangennith ❶ 01792 386669 ⓦ www.pjsurfshop.co.uk ❶ 09.00–17.30 daily ❶ Bus: 115, 116

Rhossili Gallery Very nice contemporary artwork, photography and jewellery by local and national artists and designers. ❸ The Green, Rhossili ❶ 01792 391190 ⓦ www.rhossiligallery.com ❶ 10.00–17.00 Mon–Sat, closed Sun ❶ Bus: 118, X18

TAKING A BREAK

Coffee Shop Three Cliffs £ Small coffee shop with a mouthwatering selection of cakes along with meals made using locally sourced food. ❸ Southgate, Pennard ❶ 01792 233230 ⓦ www.threecliffs.com ❶ 09.00–18.00 daily ❶ Bus: 14, 14A

The Bay Bistro & Coffee House £–££ Wonderful views across the beach accompanied by delicious home-made food and reviving

beverages. It's worth a visit in the evening to sample the fresh fish. ⓐ Rhossili ⓣ 01792 390519 ⓦ www.thebaybistro.com ⓛ 10.00–17.30, 19.00–21.00 daily ⓝ Bus: 118, X18

The King Arthur Hotel £–££ A very welcome sight if you've just walked over Cefn Bryn. Sit inside by the fire or outside in the sun to tuck into thick-cut local ham, egg and chips washed down with real ale. There's often seasonal game on the menu too. ⓐ Higher Green, Reynoldston ⓣ 01792 390775 ⓦ www.king arthurhotel.co.uk ⓛ 12.00–21.00 Mon–Thur & Sun, 12.00–21.30 Fri & Sat ⓝ Bus: 115, 118, X18

Maes-Yr-Haf ££–£££ Stylish 'restaurant with rooms', which owes its success to the inventive use of local, seasonal produce: the pan-roasted fillet of Welsh Black beef is a winner, as is the twice-baked Oxwich Point crab soufflé. There are regional ales and spirits on the drinks menu. ⓐ Parkmill ⓣ 01792 371000 ⓦ www.maes-yr-haf.com ⓛ 12.00–14.30, 19.00–21.30 daily ⓝ Bus: 117, 118, X18

AFTER DARK

The King's Head After a hard day's surfing, settle down amid the olde-worlde décor in this 17th-century pub and try a Felinfoel brew or a wee dram from their whisky collection. ⓐ Llangennith ⓣ 01792 386212 ⓦ www.kingsheadgower.co.uk ⓛ 11.00–23.00 Mon–Sat, 12.00–22.30 Sun ⓝ Bus: 115, 116

ⓞ *The Norwegian Church was built for sailors visiting from Norway*

PRACTICAL
information

Directory

GETTING THERE

By air

Swansea's nearest airport is Cardiff Airport (**a** Rhoose, Vale of Glamorgan **t** 01446 711111 **w** www.tbicardiffairport.com), which is actually just over 19 km (12 miles) west of Cardiff (60 km/ 37 miles southeast of Swansea). There is no direct public transport either to or from Swansea and it's best to continue your journey by train, taxi or hire car. The airport is mainly used by charter companies and budget airlines, including bmibaby (**t** 0905 828 2828 **w** www.bmibaby.com) and Flybe (**t** 0871 700 2000 **w** www.flybe.com). Check out **w** www.skyscanner.net for the best deals.

Many people are aware that air travel emits CO_2, which contributes to climate change. You may be interested in the possibility of lessening the environmental impact of your flight through the charity **Climate Care**, which offsets your CO_2 by funding environmental projects around the world. Visit **w** www.jpmorganclimatecare.com

By rail

The city is easily accessible by rail from all across Britain; you can travel direct to London in three hours. Contact National Rail (**t** 0845 748 4950 **w** www.nationalrail.co.uk) for further information; it's advisable to book tickets well in advance and/ or travel off peak to get the best deals. **Arriva Trains** (**t** 0845 606 1660 **w** www.arrivatrainswales.co.uk) runs local services within Wales.

By road

From the east, you'll arrive in Swansea along Fabian Way, having come off the M4 at Junction 42. **National Express** (☎ 0871 781 8178 ⓦ www.nationalexpress.com) runs direct coaches from London in about five hours; for other cities see the website. There is a swish new **Greyhound** service (☎ 0900 096 0000 ⓦ www.greyhounduk.com) from Swansea to Cardiff.

By ferry

Fastnet (☎ 0844 576 8831 ⓦ www.fastnetline.com) operates an overnight service between Swansea and Cork three times a week (Sept–June) and four times a week (June & July). **Irish Ferries** (☎ +353 818 300 400 ⓦ www.irishferries.com) sail from Pembroke Dock to Rosslare twice a day in 4 hours, and **Stena Line** (☎ 0844 770 7070 ⓦ www.stenaline.co.uk) travels from Fishguard to Rosslare twice daily in 3$\frac{1}{2}$ hours with **Stena Europe** throughout the year and in 2 hours with **Stena Express** (July & Aug).

GETTING AROUND

The buses in Swansea are operated by **First Cymru** (☎ 01792 572255 ⓦ www.firstcymru.co.uk) and depart from and arrive at the new bus station at the back of the Quadrant Centre.

Taxis can be found at the train station, St Mary's Square and The Kingsway; in the evening there are ranks on Caer Street, Newton Street, College Street and The Kingsway. **Data Cabs** (☎ 01792 474747 ⓦ www.datacabs.com) is Swansea's biggest taxi company.

Bikes can be hired from **Schmoos** (ⓐ 10 Wyndham Street ☎ 01792 467070) or **Action Bikes** (ⓐ 5 St David's Square ☎ 01792 464640).

Local car-hire companies include **Enterprise Rent-A-Car** (☎ 01792 480484 ⓦ www.enterprise.co.uk), **Day's** (☎ 0800 389 7626 ⓦ www.daysrental.co.uk) and **Avis** (☎ 0844 544 6104 ⓦ www.avis.co.uk). Compare prices at ⓦ www.carrentals.co.uk

HEALTH, SAFETY & CRIME

Like all cities, Swansea has its problems with car crime and alcohol-related incidents so it's best to hide valuables from prying eyes and keep your wits about you at night. If you're staying at a hotel, keep one of their business cards on your person in case of emergency or if you get lost. Women travelling alone should check that they're getting into a licensed taxi (black with round yellow stickers on the doors). In an emergency, ring ☎ 999 or dial ☎ 101 for non-emergencies.

MEDICAL SERVICES

NHS Direct (☎ 0845 4647 ⓦ www.nhsdirect.wales.nhs.uk) will advise on whether you need to see a doctor or dentist, where you can get medical attention and where you can find a pharmacy at any hour of the day. **Morriston Hospital** (ⓐ Morriston ☎ 01792 702222) is the nearest place to go for A&E treatment.

OPENING HOURS

Most shops open from 09.00 to 17.30 Monday to Saturday and some high-street brands also open on Sunday from 11.00 to 17.00. If you fancy a midnight feast, Tesco Marina (ⓐ Albert Row, Oystermouth Road) is open for 24 hours from Tuesday to Saturday. Most banks open 09.00 to 17.00 Monday to Friday and some open from 10.00 to 16.00 on Saturday.

TOILETS

There are manned public toilets by the Quadrant Station, Welcome Lane (at the side of Argos) and Caer Street (next to the Cross Keys pub), which all have baby changing facilities. There are also toilets on the first floor of the Quadrant Shopping Centre.

CHILDREN

Swansea has plenty to occupy children, what with all the beaches in summer and the wide variety of outdoor activities on offer, not to mention indoor attractions like the National Waterfront Museum, Plantasia and the LC; the boating lake at Singleton Park is also a popular destination. The city centre is safe and easy enough to navigate with little ones but it's advisable to take care when crossing busy thoroughfares like The Kingsway and Oystermouth Road.

TRAVELLERS WITH DISABILITIES

These days, the majority of buildings are much more readily accessible, and getting around by public transport shouldn't be a problem as most of First Cymru's buses can lower their chassis to allow on wheelchairs (and pushchairs). The Quadrant Shopping Centre hires out wheelchairs for free, as does Shopmobility (ⓐ Unit 12, St David's Centre ☎ 01792 461785 🕐 09.00–16.30 Mon–Sat, closed Sun).

FURTHER INFORMATION

Swansea Tourist Information Centre ⓐ Plymouth Street (near Quadrant Bus Station) ☎ 01792 468321 🌐 www.visitswansea bay.com 🕐 09.30–17.30 Mon–Sat, 10.00–16.00 Sun (July–Sept)

A

A Space in the City 25
accommodation 22–5
airports 32, 90
Alexander, The 24
Amis, Sir Kingsley 68
annual events 8–9
art galleries 12, 45–6, 60, 68
Arthur's Stone 82
arts *see* culture
attractions
 city centre 42–5
 free 30
 Gower Peninsula 82–4
 Mumbles 75–6
 Swansea West 64–6
 top 26–7
 waterfront 54–7
 wet weather 31

B

B&B 22, 24–5
banks 92
Bay Bistro & Coffee House 87–8
Beachcomber, The 24
beaches 80
Beau Nash House 44
bike hire 91
Botanical Gardens 66
Bouchon de Rossi 50–51
Brangwyn Hall 30, 66, 68
Burry Holms 82
buses 37, 84, 91
bushcraft 86

C

Café Two-Cann 60–61
Café Valance 77
cafés 49–50, 60–62, 69–70, 77–8, 87–8
car hire 38, 92
castle ruins 42
Castle Square 42
Cefn Bryn 82
Ceri Richards Gallery 68
Charlie's 62
Chattery, The 72
children 93
churches 46–7, 55
cinemas 12, 31, 53

city areas
 city centre 40, 42–53
 Swansea West 40, 64–72
 waterfront 6, 15, 40, 54–63
city centre 40, 42–53
climate 8
Climate Care 90
clubs 18, 53, 72, 79
Clyne Gardens 26, 64
coaches 36, 91
Coffee Shop Three Cliffs 87
comedy venues 46, 72
Constitution Hill 64–5
cricket 20
crime 36, 92
Cross Keys 44
culture 12
 city centre 45–7
 Swansea West 68
 waterfront 57–9
Cwmdonkin Park 65
cycling 30, 38, 80, 91

D

directory 90–3
disabilities, travellers with 93
Doctor Who 54
Dragon, The 23
Dragon Brasserie 51
driving 32–3, 38, 91, 92
Dylan Thomas Birthplace 25
Dylan Thomas Centre 12, 26, 57
Dylan Thomas Prize 58
Dylan Thomas Theatre 12, 58

E

eating and drinking 16–17
 city centre 49–53
 Gower Peninsula 87–8
 Mumbles 77–9
 Swansea West 69–72
 waterfront 60–63
Egypt Centre, The 68
entertainment 18–19
Environment Centre 60

F

farmers' market 76
ferries 36, 91

festivals 8–9, 30, 80
film festival 8
food specialties 16–17, 27
football 20
free attractions 30
Fresco 61

G

Gallini's 62
Garage, The 72
Georgian Swansea 54–5
Glynn Vivian Art Gallery 12, 45–6
golf 20, 86
Govinda's 49–50
Gower Coast Adventures 74
Gower Heritage Centre 84
Gower Peninsula 7, 22, 30, 80–88
Grand, The 23
Grand Theatre 12, 46
Guildhall 66, 68

H

Hanson at the Chelsea Café 52
health 92
Heseltine, Michael 68
history 10–11, 48
Holbrook's 50
Home from Home 25
horseriding 86
hostel 22
hotels 22–4

I

Ice House, The 61–2
itineraries 28–9

J

jazz 72
Joe's 69

J

Kardomah 50, 51
King Arthur Hotel 88
King's Head 88
Kitchen Table 77

L

La Braseria 52
La Parrilla 63
Langland Brasserie 78
LC (leisure centre) 21, 31

Leonardo's 24
Liberty Stadium 7, 18, 20
Llangennith 27, 82

M
Maes-Yr-Haf 88
Mamma Mia 51
maps 34–5, 41, 81
    symbols 4
Maritime Quarter 55
market, indoor 14, 16, 17, 27, 48–9
medical services 92
Meridian Tower 55
Milkwoodjam 53
Mirador Town House 25
Monkey Café 52
Morgans Hotel 23, 55, 63
mountain boarding 86
Mumbles 7, 22, 26, 30, 74–9
Mumbles Hill Nature Reserve 75
Mumbles Lighthouse 75
Mumbles Pier 75
museums 12, 26, 30, 58–9, 68, 84
music hall 44
music, live 12, 18, 53, 66, 72

N
National Showcaves Centre for Wales 31
National Waterfront Museum 12, 26, 58
Nick Holly Gallery 60
nightlife 18–19
    city centre 52–3
    Swansea West 72
    waterfront 63
No Sign Bar 52
Norton House Hotel 79
Norwegian Church 55, 60

O
Oceana 18, 53
One Shoe Café 69
opening hours 92
orientation 36–7
out of town
    Gower Peninsula 7, 22, 30, 80–88

Mumbles 7, 22, 26, 30, 74–9
Oystermouth Castle 76

P
Palace Theatre 44
Pant-y-Gwydr 71
parking 33
parks and gardens 26, 64, 65, 66
PA's 79
Plantasia 31
pottery 46
prices 4
Promenade 27, 54
public transport 37
pubs and bars 44, 52–3, 63, 71–2, 88

Q
Queen's, The 63

R
rainfall 8, 31
restaurants 50–52, 62–3, 70–71, 78–9
Rhossili 17, 27, 30, 82–3
road, arriving by 32–3, 91
rugby union 20

S
SA1 55
safety 36, 92
Sail Bridge 57
St Cenydd's 82
Saint David's Week 8
St Mary's Church 46–7
seasons 8
self-catering 22, 25
Shed, The 70
shopping 14–15, 48–9, 60, 69, 76, 87, 92
Sin City 53
Singleton Park 66
Slice 71
sport and relaxation 20–21, 86
Surf Club 79
surfing 27, 80, 86, 87
Swansea Jazzland 72
Swansea Museum 12, 59
Swansea Observatory 57

Swansea West 40, 64–72
swimming pool 21

T
Taliesin Arts Centre 12, 68
taxis 91, 92
tennis 21
tenpin bowling 31
Thai Elephant, The 62
theatres 12, 46, 58
Thomas, Dylan 5, 7, 9, 12, 51, 57, 58, 59, 65, 66
Three Cliffs Bay 83
toilets 93
tourist information 93
Towers, The 23–4
trains 90
travel
    to Swansea 32–3, 36, 90–91
    within Swansea 37–8, 91–2
Truffle 70
Ty Tawe 47

U
Uplands 18, 22, 64, 65, 68
Uplands Tavern 71

V
Verdi's 78
Viceroy of India 70

W
Walkabout 53
walking 30, 80
Wasabi 70
waterfront 6, 15, 40, 54–63
watersports 21, 80
Weobley Castle 83–4
Westbourne, The 71–2
wet-weather attractions 31
White House, The 24–5
White Rose 79
Wild Swan 50
Wind Street 6–7, 45
Windsor Lodge 22–3
Worms Head 74, 82–3

Z
Zeta-Jones, Catherine 6, 11, 74

ACKNOWLEDGEMENTS
The photographs in this book were taken by Grant Rooney for Thomas Cook Publishing, to whom the copyright belongs, except for the following:
National Waterfront Museum page 7.

Project editor: Rosalind Munro
Proofreaders: Ceinwen Sinclair & Michele Greenbank
Layout: Donna Pedley
Indexer: Marie Lorimer

AUTHOR BIOGRAPHY
A member of the British Guild of Travel Writers, Victoria Trott (www.victoriatrott.co.uk) was born, brought up and still lives in the Swansea area. She writes and revises travel guides for major publishers and contributes features to national consumer magazines.

Send your thoughts to
books@thomascook.com

- Found a great bar, club, shop or must-see sight that we don't feature?
- Like to tip us off about any information that needs a little updating?
- Want to tell us what you love about this handy little guidebook and more importantly how we can make it even handier?

Then here's your chance to tell all! Send us ideas, discoveries and recommendations today and then look out for your valuable input in the next edition of this title.

Email the above address (stating the title) or write to:
pocket guides Series Editor, Thomas Cook Publishing, PO Box 227, Coningsby Road, Peterborough PE3 8SB, UK.